S0-ARM-150

Introduction to
THEOLOGY

John D. Laurance, S.J., Editor
Department of Theology, Marquette University

Pearson
Custom
Publishing

Cover Image: Assumption of the Virgin, by Titian. © Scala/Firenze.

Images:
Part 1:   *Adam and Eve,* by Lucas Cranach the Elder. © Scala/Art
          Resource, NY
Part II: *St. Augustine,* by Marco Zoppo. © National Gallery, London.
Part III: "Assumption of the Virgin" by Titian. © Scala/Firenze

Copyright © 2000 by John D. Laurance, S.J.
All rights reserved.

This copyright covers material written expressly for this volume by
the editor/s as well as the compilation itself. It does not cover the
individual selections herein that first appeared elsewhere. Permission
to reprint these has been obtained by Pearson Custom Publishing for
this edition only. Further reproduction by any means, electronic or
mechanical, including photocopying and recording, or by any information storage or retrieval system, must be arranged with the
individual copyright holders noted.

Printed in the United States of America

10 9 8 7 6 5 4 3

Please visit our web site at www.pearsoncustom.com

ISBN 0–536–61000–2

BA 992221

PEARSON CUSTOM PUBLISHING
75 Arlington Street, Boston, MA 02116
A Pearson Education Company

Copyright Acknowledgments

Grateful acknowledgment is made to the following sources for permission to reprint material copyrighted or controlled by them:

"Nicene-Constantinopolitan Creed," by Henry Denzinger, reprinted from *Sources of Catholic Dogma,* 1957, translated by Roy J. Deferrari, Herder & Herder.

Excerpts from "Confessions: Book Eight," by Augustine of Hippo, reprinted from *Confessions of St. Augustine,* 1943, translated by Frank J. Sheed. Copyright © by Frank J. Sheed and Ward.

"Summa Theologiae, I, Q. 1, art. 1: Is Theology Necessary?" by Thomas Aquinas, reprinted from *O.P. Summa Theologica,* by Fathers of the English Dominican Province, Benziger Publishing Company.

"Revelations of Divine Love, 58-60," by Julian of Norwich, reprinted from *Revelations of Divine Love,* 1982, translated by Clifton Wolters, Penguin Books, Ltd. Copyright © 1982 by Clifton Wolters.

"On Christian Freedom," by Martin Luther, reprinted from *A History of Christianity,* 1985, edited by Clyde L. Manschreck, Prentice-Hall, Inc.

Excerpts from *Rerum Novarum,* by Pope Leo XIII, 1891, Pauline Books & Media.

"Letter from a Birmingham Jail," by Dr. Martin Luther King, Jr., reprinted from *A Testament of Hope: The Essential Writings of Martin Luther King, Jr.,* 1958. Copyright © 1958 by Martin Luther King, Jr., renewed 1986 by Coretta Scott King. Reprinted by arrangement with the Heirs to the Estate of Martin Luther King, Jr., c/o Writer's House, Inc.

In every individual human being everything is present (homo quo-dammodo omnia), and the whole achieves a unique manifestation of itself in each particular individual. The community of humankind for its part is not the agglomeration of the many—all too many, but the unity in love of those each of whom is unique in his or her own right, a love which sets each free for his own, which assembles all this and so once more unifies it.[1]

—Karl Rahner, S.J. (1904–1984)

[1] Karl Rahner, "Marriage as a Sacrament," pp. 199–221 in: *Theological Investi-gations*, X, David Bourke, Tr. (New York: Seabury, 1977), p. 210. English rendered gender inclusive—Ed.

Introduction

During the 1994–95 academic year, Marquette University's Department of Theology held a series of meetings to redesign its basic undergraduate course, "THEOLOGY 001: Introduction to Theology." This reformulation was undertaken (a) to provide incoming students with an awareness of the key personages, events, and concepts, as well as the overall historical development, of the Catholic and wider Christian traditions; and by doing so (b) to furnish the common background presupposed in all other theology courses at Marquette. Since no textbook available at the time was thought capable of achieving these goals, the department decided to choose readings from the Bible and church tradition and gather them into a common text to be used by all sections of the introductory course.

Obviously the biblical and ecclesial heritage from which these readings had to be chosen is dauntingly huge, and so any selection would necessarily be very limited. However, because the department's actual choice represents a wide spectrum of theological sources across the whole span of sacred history, it offers a surprisingly comprehensive introduction to theology. Nor does a proper use of the book demand that all the readings be covered or studied in the precise order in which they appear. As a study in specifically *Christian* theology, its unity derives from the person, words and actions of Jesus Christ, so that its cardinal, defining selection is the Gospel of Mark. All other readings can be found either to anticipate or burgeon forth from this fundamental New Testament understanding of Christ as the culmination and fullness of God's self-revelation in human history. Within this christological unity, then, each instructor is free to arrange the readings, and supplement them with other background material, according to his or her own theological synthesis.

One might, for example, begin with the Aquinas reading (#13) since it explains how theology is a unique academic discipline or "doctrine," that is, kind of *teaching*. Proceeding then to Vatican II, the very last reading in the book (#20), one would discover how the God studied in theology is to be found, not as one object among others whose existence could be "proved" or studied in itself, but as Someone who calls human beings by name, and who, therefore, can be known only in personal response in faith to that call. The fact that God has always "spoken" in this way to human beings, in self-revelation, first through the prophets of old and then fully in Christ (sacramentally active now in the Church and especially in its liturgical response of faith), offers a comprehensive theological perspective from which to read all the other readings, from Genesis to Dr. Martin Luther King, Jr.

Or one might prefer a law/gospel approach to the readings. In Exodus the Mosaic law is presented as a sign of God's providence. In Galatians, however, St. Paul warns against trying to earn salvation by keeping the law. As a result, what salutary role law might have in Christian life has been a question throughout the centuries, as is evident in the Martin Luther and Martin Luther King, Jr., readings.

Another possible path is Christian typology: tracing through the readings how—on the basis of the New Testament itself—the fullness of God's word, Jesus Christ, is savingly present throughout salvation history both before and after his historical life on earth,[2] making it

---

[2] For a brief explanation of this belief, along with indications of its presence throughout Christian tradition, see Jack Wintz, "Christ, the Head of Creation," *America*, Sept.,14 1996, 22–23.

possible for "*all* human beings to be saved and come to a knowledge of the truth" (1 Timothy 2:4) since "there is no salvation through anyone else, nor is there any other name under heaven by which we are to be saved" (Acts 4:12). Here the 1 Corinthians 10–15 reading (#7) is key, indicating how God acted through Moses and water from the rock in the desert as saving types of Christ (c. 10); and how Adam himself, in whom for St. Paul the whole of humanity was present, foreshadowed the mystery of Christ, the new Adam, in whose bodily self-offering on the cross is realized a new humanity (c. 15). The brief descriptions of the readings found in the Table of Contents, as well as the "Introductions" to some other selections, indicate further typological connections.

Other traceable theological topics are: (1) creation, new creation and the sacramental world; (2) sin, grace, and conversion; (3) discipleship, service, and suffering; (4) church, baptism, and Eucharist; and (5) communal and personal prayer.

As editor I am particularly indebted to those members of the Department of Theology at Marquette who, with generosity and expertise, composed the fuller introductions to readings throughout the book, and whose names appear subscribed to their respective compositions.

John D. Laurance, S.J., Ph.D.
Department of Theology
Marquette University
March 25, 2000

Contents

      These Pentateuch selections include narrations on cre-
ation, humankind's fall from grace, the origins of Israel,
God's leading his chosen people to freedom, manna from
heaven, bestowal of the law and the covenant sacrifice. For
the New Testament these accounts foreshadow humanity's
new creation and redemption in Christ who is the new
Adam (I Corinthians 15), the new Moses (Matthew 5–7)
and the "Bread of Life"(John 6); the Church as the new
People of God (I Peter); and the Eucharist as fulfillment of
the covenant (Mark 14).

      This brief passage makes the kingship of Israel, in the per-
son of King David, a metaphor and promise of the future
Messiah, whom the New Testament identifies as Jesus
(Mark 10:47), who inaugurates and embodies God's kingdom on earth (Mark 1:14).

body, his church (c. 12), a new humanity (c. 15). Baptism and Eucharist are seen as fulfillments of Old Testament types (c. 10) and effective only if celebrated as part of an overall life of loving service (c. 11).

ST. AUGUSTINE OF HIPPO (354–430):

St. Augustine was a North African bishop and theologian
whose primary concerns were the interplay between God's
grace and human freedom, and the call to salvation. No
other single theologian has exercised as decisive an influence on the shape and character of western theology, both
Catholic and Protestant. The *Confessions*, Augustine's
grateful account before God of his adult faith conversion,
is a classic of western spirituality.

COUNCIL OF NICAEA II (787):

Since its beginnings the Church struggled against those
who claimed that, because God is Spirit, the material
world is unable to mediate God's presence. This seventh
ecumenical council affirms once-for-all that, just as Christ
is the saving "image (*eikōn*) of the invisible God" (Colossians 1:15), so does Christ continue to save humankind
through the institutional Church and its faith-expression
in physical sacraments and sacred images.

ST. THOMAS AQUINAS (1225–1274):

A Dominican priest, St. Thomas of Aquino (Italy)
employed the Bible, Aristotelian philosophy and the wisdom of his theological predecessors in creating a Christian
theology that dominated Catholic self-understanding up
to the twentieth century. Transformed in the work of Karl
Rahner, Bernard Lonergan and others, "Thomism" continues to be highly influential. This introductory question
taken from Thomas' tripartite *Summa theologiae* ("Com-
pendium of Theology") reflects in disputational form on
the role of theology as a "science."

JULIAN OF NORWICH (CA. 1342–1420):

An English mystic, Julian lived a life of solitude as an
anchoress next to a church in Norwich, East Anglia. At

30, while near death, she received sixteen mystical visions on the passion of Christ, the Trinity, the love of God, the Incarnation, redemption, sin, and divine consolation, many of which are described in her work, *Revelations of Divine Love.* Julian represents one traditional type of Christian mysticism: the way of imaging God by the use of imagination or words (kataphatic), as distinct from the way of imagelessness, stillness, and wordlessness (apophatic).

MARTIN LUTHER (1483–1546):

Martin Luther was a German biblical theologian and one-time Augustinian priest whose activities and writings were catalysts for the Protestant Reformation. His translation of the Bible into vernacular German opened up the riches of Scripture to the masses. Luther was active as pastor, preacher, teacher, and leader in the churches of the Reformation until his death in 1546. In 1520 he published "On the Freedom of the Christian," in which he argues that salvation comes by faith alone and that, since priesthood consists in the ability through faith to pray for others, all Christians are equally priests.

IGNATIUS OF LOYOLA (1491–1566)

IGNATIUS OF LOYOLA (1491–1566)

In his *Autobiography* Ignatius of Loyola, of a Basque noble family, details how he was inspired to leave all for Christ during recuperation from a cannonball injury. Graced later with deep experiences of prayer, he capsuled the profound dynamic of the gospel into four "weeks" of meditations called *The Spiritual Exercises.* These he used to guide others to find God's presence and will in their lives. In the process he attracted around him a company of men which Pope Paul III approved to be a religious order of priests and brothers in the Church (1540): the Society of Jesus, known as "The Jesuits."

POPE LEO XIII (1810–1903):

Called the "Magna Carta" of Catholic social teaching, this nineteenth-century papal encyclical responds to the inhuman economic and social conditions created by the unfettered Industrial Age. Using philosophical reasoning in light of Revelation, Leo XIII presents the Church's understanding of the dignity of the human person, the sacredness and inviolability of the family, the right to private property and the proper relationship between capital and labor. The encyclical echoes faith teachings found in previous readings in this book, especially in regard to true discipleship, the unity of the human race in Christ, and God's intended use of the created world by human beings.

DR. MARTIN LUTHER KING, JR (1929–1968):

Martin Luther King, Jr., was an African-American Baptist minister and theologian who became leader of the U.S. civil rights movement for racial justice from the mid-1950s until his assassination in 1968 at the age of 39. "Letter from a Birmingham Jail," written while imprisoned for participating in civil rights demonstrations, expresses many of King's core convictions, especially that the African-American struggle for freedom and equality is part of the overall call to Christian discipleship, and that non-violent direct action is the best means of exposing injustice and bringing about societal change.

THE SECOND VATICAN COUNCIL (1962–1965):

Pope John XXIII summoned Vatican II to "update" the Catholic Church. After setting forth principles for internal renewal, the council taught the Church to see God's presence in the wider world, especially in other Christian denominations and non-Christian religions. Its initial document, *Sacrosanctum Concilium*, declares that the Church's liturgy is "the fountain and summit" of its life in Christ.

This "Constitution on the Sacred Liturgy" is a direct result of the "liturgical movement" that began in 1909 as a widespread effort of Catholic scholars, pastors, and laity to rediscover the connection between liturgy with the rest of Christian life, focusing especially on how in the liturgy Christ acts in his Paschal Mystery through the faith-participation of all the members of the Church.

Time Line

B.C. (B.C.E.)—*B.C. dates are mostly approximate:*

1800	Abraham
1250	The Exodus
1000	King David
950	*J* (Yahwist source for **Genesis, Exodus**)
850	*E* (Elohist source for **Genesis, Exodus**)
742–701	Isaiah
722	Fall of the Northern Kingdom
650	**2 Samuel 7**
650	*D* (Deuteronomist source for **Genesis, Exodus**)
620	King Josiah's Reform
587–537	Fall of Southern Kingdom, Temple destroyed; Babylonian Exile
550	Second Isaiah (**Isaiah 40–55**)
550	*P* (Priestly source for **Genesis, Exodus**)
563–483	Siddhartha Gautama, the "Buddha"
551–479	Confucius, Chinese Philosopher
470–399	Socrates, Greek Philosopher
450	Editing of **Isaiah 1–12**
427–347	Plato, Greek Philosopher
384–322	Aristotle, Greek Philosopher

A.D. (C.E.):

ca. 4 B.C.–A.D. 30	*JESUS*
ca. 46–58	St. Paul's three missionary journeys
ca. 54	St. Paul, **Letter to the Galatians**
ca. 55	St. Paul, **First Letter to the Corinthians**
ca. 64	Sts. Peter and Paul martyred in Rome
70	Destruction of the Temple in Jerusalem
ca. 70	**Gospel of Mark**
ca. 70–100	Four **Gospels**
ca. 100–165	St. Justin Martyr, **The First Apology**
ca. 120–200	St. Irenaeus, bishop, theologian, first Patristic writer
ca. 170–236	St. Hippolytus of Rome, **The Apostolic Tradition**
ca. 185–254	Origen, priest, theologian
ca. 290–347	St. Pachomius, founder of coenobitic monasticism
313	The Edict of Milan
325	Council of Nicaea, rejection of Arianism
ca. 330–95	Sts. Basil the Great, Gregory Nazianzen, Gregory of Nyssa
381	Council of Constantinople I, **Nicene-Constantinopolitan Creed**
339–397	St. Ambrose of Milan, bishop, theologian
345–420	St. Jerome, the Latin "Vulgate" Bible
347–407	St. John Chrysostom, Patriarch of Constantinople, theologian
354–430	St. Augustine, bishop, theologian; 397–401 **The Confessions**
431	Council of Ephesus, rejection of Nestorianism
?–461	Pope St. Leo I, "the Great," 440–461
451	Council of Chalcedon, rejection of Monophysitism
ca. 480–ca. 550	St. Benedict, "Father of Western Monasticism"
ca. 540–604	Pope St. Gregory I, "the Great," 590–604

570–632	Muhammad, founder of Islam
787	Council of Nicaea II, **Against Iconoclasm**
800	Charlemagne crowned Holy Roman Emperor
927–1156	The Cluniac Reform
1054	Eastern Orthodox-Catholic Schism begins
1033–1109	St. Anselm of Canterbury, bishop, theologian
1090–1153	St. Bernard of Clairvaux, Cistercian mystic and reformer
ca. 1100–1160	Peter Lombard, Master of the "Sentences"
1170–1221	St. Dominic, founder of the Order of Preachers
1181–1226	St. Francis of Assisi, founder of the Friars Minor
1225–1274	St. Thomas Aquinas, O.P., **Summa theologiae**
1342–1420	Julian of Norwich, **Revelations of Divine Love**
1347–1380	St. Catherine of Siena, Dominican mystic, papal counselor
1378–1417	Great Western Schism
1483–1546	Martin Luther, 1520 **Freedom of the Christian**
1517	Beginning of the Protestant Reformation
1509–1564	John Calvin, Protestant reformer
1491–1556	St. Ignatius of Loyola, **Autobiography, Spiritual Exercises**
1540	Founding of the Society of Jesus
1506–1552	St. Francis Xavier, Jesuit, "Apostle of the Indies"
1545–1563	Council of Trent
1570	Missal of Pope St. Pius V: Tridentine Mass
1515–1582	St. Teresa of Avila, Carmelite mystic
1596–1650	René Descartes, French Philosopher
1724–1804	Immanuel Kant, German Philosopher
1790	John Carroll consecrated first Catholic bishop in the U.S.
1869–1870	Vatican Council I declares papal infallibility
1810–1903	Pope Leo XIII, 1891 **"Rerum Novarum,"** first social encyclical
1909	Beginning of the "Liturgical Movement"

1876–1958	Pope Pius XII (Eugenio Pacelli), 1943 "Mystici Corporis," 1943 "Divino Afflante Spiritu," 1947 "Mediator Dei"
1886–1948	Dom Odo Casel, O.S.B., theologian
1939–1945	The Second World War
1947–1960	Dead Sea Scrolls discovered
1948	World Council of Churches established
1929–1968	Martin Luther King, Jr., 1963 **Letter from a Birmingham Jail**
1962–1965	Vatican Council II, 1963 **Constitution on Sacred Liturgy**
1965	Patriarch Athenagoras I (1886–1972) and Pope Paul VI (1897–1978) jointly deplore the mutual anathemas of 1054.
1969	Missal of Pope Paul VI
1904–1984	Karl Rahner, S.J., theologian
1999	Catholic/Lutheran Agreement on Justification by Faith

I
Introductions to Biblical Readings

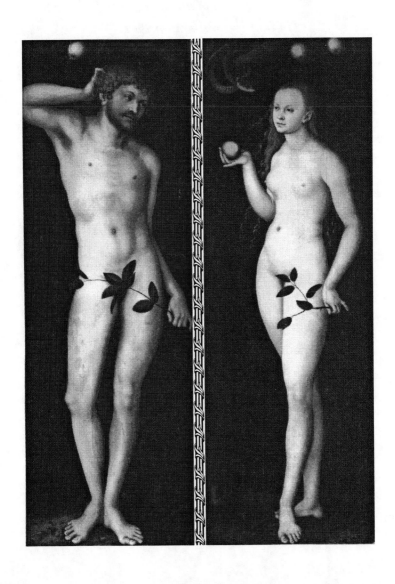

He is the image of the invisible God,
the first-born of all creatures.
In him everything in heaven
and on earth was created,
things visible and invisible,
whether thrones or dominations,
principalities or powers;
all were created through him, and for him.
He is before all else that is.
In him everything continues in being.
It is he who is head of the body, the church;
he who is the beginning, the first-born of the dead,
so that primacy may be his in everything.
It pleased God to make absolute fullness reside in him
and, by means of him, to reconcile everything
in his person, both on earth and in the heavens,
making peace through the blood of his cross.

Colossians 1:15–20

1

Genesis 1–24 and Exodus 1–34

The first five books of the Bible are known as the Pentateuch (the 5-scroll). They are the work of several authors (including J, the Yahwist; E, the Elohist; and P, the Priestly writer) stretching over about 450 years, beginning in the middle 900s B.C. during Solomon's reign and edited together finally around 500 B.C.

"THE COVENANT FORMULA"

According to the "Covenant Formula" that permeates the final author's combination of J, E, and P, their "redaction," human beings are consistently tempted to "be like gods." The only victory possible over this temptation and its destructive results is union with the real God by way of the Promise and then the Covenant. This pattern of the "Covenant Formula" is unfolded in the Bible in concentric circles which can be detected if one begins by reading Deuteronomy 26; goes next to Joshua 24; then to Exodus; proceeds on to the Genesis story of Abraham; and finally to the cycle of stories leading up to Abraham illustrating the need for the Promise (Adam and Eve, Cain and Abel, the Flood, the Tower of Babel).

3

HISTORICAL STORIES?

These stories were formed over the centuries as part of liturgical celebrations, faith-responses to God's past saving deeds. They are expressed very imaginatively in order to convey to later generations the lived experience of God's saving actions. Consequently, in reading these accounts one must be aware of what literary form the authors are using. To discern the meaning in the sometimes poetic expression, keep in mind these four presuppositions:

1. *The author **meant** something:* It is necessary to suspend disbelief until one finds what the author has in mind by investigating the use of words, the historical, cultural situation behind the text, and the like.

2. *The author **knew** what he meant:* This is to avoid the false problem of how much the prophets knew: they obviously intended a meaning within their own historical situation, but did they know what use would be made of their texts later, what deeper truths about sacred history would be found in them? It is not necessary that they know this. It is also highly unlikely.

3. *The author tried to **say** what he meant:* What are the modes of discourse, the literary forms being used? Here examples from literature are a great help. Homer, fairy tales, Shakespeare, comics are all rich and known examples of creations which tell "truth" without necessarily being tied to "facts."

4. *The author tried to say it **to someone**:* One says things differently to different audiences and to the same audience in different circumstances. What is the historical context of the text?

OTHER PENTATEUCHAL THEMES

To understand better Genesis and Exodus, notice some additional themes:

1. **Displacement—Younger Son:** God's gifts undeserved.
2. **Murmuring:** The people's continual discontent and lack of faith.
3. **Law:** Part of God's covenant, a source of blessings.
4. **Signs of the Covenant:** Rainbow, circumcision, sabbath.

—*Rev. Thomas A. Caldwell, S.J.*

2

2 Samuel 7

BACKGROUND

2 Samuel, one of the historical books of the Bible, concentrates mostly on King David's reign in Jerusalem, during the 10th century B.C. The story of David starts in 1 Samuel where the origins of monarchy as an institution in Israel are presented. 1 Samuel begins by illustrating with stories the Israelites' desire for a king, then it moves to the selection of Saul as king, his fall from favor, the choice of David as the Lord's anointed or "**messiah**," and finally the struggle between Saul and David over the leadership of Israel. 2 Samuel opens with the defeat and death of Saul for whom David mourns, and then it moves into chapters about David's military and political successes: David (a) unites the 12 tribes who proclaim him king, (b) conquers Jerusalem as his capital (chapter 5), and (c) brings in the religious relics from the desert experience: the Ark of the Covenant and the Tent of Meeting, relics that had been the focal point for the worship of the LORD during the time of the settlement, 1200-1000 BC. These chapters all form the backdrop to 2 Samuel 7.

DAVIDIC COVENANT

Chapter Seven begins with a statement about David's desire to build a temple for the LORD—he has brought in the religious relics from the desert experience, the Ark of the Covenant and the Tent of Meeting, but he wishes to construct a permanent focal point for the worship of the 12 tribes. His prophet, Nathan, at first tells him that this is a good plan but later rescinds the LORD's permission. In the oracle delivered by Nathan, David is told that he is not to build a "house" for the LORD—the LORD will build a "house" for David! There is a wordplay here: "house" is used in both the sense of permanent structure and of a dynasty, progeny to continue David's line. The text assures that David's dynasty will continue as the chosen agent of God's salvation. This text is the basis for the tradition of the **Davidic covenant**, the tradition that God has made a covenant with his anointed, with David.

A **covenant**, in the Bible, has the particular meaning of an agreement, a bond, forged between God and His people or God and one individual. In the Old Testament books preceding 2 Samuel, we have already encountered mention of the **Abrahamic covenant**, the covenant God made with Abraham (Gen 12, 15, 17), and the **Sinai**, or **Mosaic covenant**, the agreement forged between God and the people of Israel, with Moses acting as the representative of the people. According to 2 Samuel 7, God has made a special covenant with David. David is promised two things: land and dynasty. David had wanted to build a "house" (a temple) for God; God announces, through the authoritative voice of the prophet Nathan, that He will build a "house" (a dynasty) for David. A descendent of David will always be on the throne in Jerusalem. God commits himself to David—the covenant is an eternal one, one which cannot be broken.

The importance and strength of this tradition, this idea that God has made special promises to David, is evident throughout the Old Testament: Isaiah 2:2–4; Isaiah 8:23–9:6; Isaiah 11:1–9; Psalms 2; 72. The promise of a dynasty to David becomes the basis for the messianic expectation, the hope for a messiah, that develops after the destruction of Jerusalem and the end of the Davidic dynasty in 586 B.C.

STRUCTURE

2 Samuel 7 has two parts: (1) an "oracle," in verses 1–17, and (2) David's prayer, in verses 18–29.

1. **History of the Oracle (1–17):**

   a. **The Court of Solomon (10th century B.C.).** David's desire to build a temple for the LORD. His prophet Nathan at first tells him that this is a good plan.

   b. **Prophetic Revision (9th century B.C.).** The Davidic Covenant: David is then told by Nathan that he is not to build a "house" for the LORD—the LORD will build a "house" for David!

   c. **Deuteronomistic Final Redaction (7th–6th centuries B.C.).** David's plan to build a house is interpreted within the whole scope of the Deuteronomistic view of history. The "ups and downs" (2 Samuel 7:14) of the Davidic line are tied to the successive Davidic kings' fidelity to God.

2. **David's Prayer (18–29):** An early prayer connected with the Ark ceremony is later redacted as a prayer to invoke God's blessing on the royal house of David.

SIGNIFICANCE

For Christians 2 Samuel 7 is one of the most theologically important texts in the Bible. The **Davidic covenant** first presented here is of central importance in the New Testament. Jesus is the son "descended from David according to the flesh" (Paul's Letter to the Romans, 1:3). When Christians proclaim that Jesus is **Christ (= Messiah)**, they are

affirming their belief that the **Davidic covenant** has reached its culmination in Jesus. See, e.g., Mark 8:29: "And [Jesus] asked them, 'But
who do you say that I am?' Peter said to him in reply, 'You are the
Messiah'."

— Dr. Deirdre A. Dempsey

3

Isaiah 1–12

A "CLASSICAL PROPHET"

The Book of Isaiah is one of the prophetic books in the Hebrew Bible/Old Testament. Isaiah belongs to the "classical prophets," those prophets whose words are collected into books that bear their names. Classical prophecy begins in the eighth century, after the time of the great prophet Elijah. There are four such prophets in the eighth century: Amos and Hosea in the Northern Kingdom and Isaiah and Micah in the Southern Kingdom. As background for understanding their writings it is important to know that, although the two kingdoms of Israel (the North) and Judah (the South) were thriving in the mid-eighth century, in 722 the Assyrians ended the slow collapse of the North by destroying the capital of Samaria.

"FIRST ISAIAH"

Prophetic books typically grew and were modified over centuries. First, the prophet made his pronouncements; later, individuals collected some of the sayings and wrote them down; and later still, scribes modified the collected words by expanding, editing, and applying them to life-situations of subsequent generations. Biblical scholars became aware only gradually that the text of Isaiah underwent expansion over time, not only by added written comments from others on the prophet's words, but also by large supplements to the end of the book. Thus, scholars have, for almost 100 years, identified three major sections of Isaiah, namely, chapters 1 to 39, 40 to 55, 56 to 66. Within Isaiah 1–39, often called "First Isaiah," there are also smaller, noteworthy groupings: 1–12, 13–23, 24–27, 28–33, 34–35, and 36–39. Other divisions are sometimes offered.

Chapters 1–12 form a kind of unit with a beginning and end: An introduction (c. 1); a hymn of praise and joy for God's past activity, bringing this stage of the drama to success (c. 12). Chapter 1 functions also an introduction to the whole book of Isaiah. The final editing of the entire book of Isaiah, probably in the fifth century B.C.E., is geared to encourage the reader of that time to realize that God is going to establish worldwide divine sovereignty over all nations beginning from Zion, with Zion remaining as its center.

Chapter 1, then, sets the stage for this drama by presenting the infidelity and sinfulness of the people, and also the need for punishment and purification as the ultimate preparation for this universal reign of God. Chapter 2:2–5, as a dramatic prefiguring of this fulfillment yet to come, presents Jerusalem/Zion as the elevated center of this reign. But the remaining verses of this chapter, as well as chapters 3–4, accuse the people of various aspects of infidelity and explain the threatened results of their unfaithful behavior.

SIGNIFICANCE OF ISAIAH TODAY

The twentieth century interpreter must discover what significance the original purpose of the entire book holds for people today. Many things in human thought and religious experience have occurred since that time. Today's potential meaning of biblical texts is not limited to the intention of the authors who produced them. Yet specific parts of the book of Isaiah, because it is a collection, can be read on their own so that one can find the meaning of a passage both within its original setting and within the contemporary community of faith.

Christian theology has sometimes isolated for reflection those passages where the book anticipates the fulfillment of the promise of a Davidic dynasty (announced in 2 Samuel 7 and echoed in Psalm 89), namely Isaiah 7:14, 9:6–7, and 11:1–9. Many readers see the experience of the prophet in chapter 6 as a precise example of the core religious experience of awe.

—*Dr. John J. Schmitt*

4
Isaiah 40–55

These chapters of Isaiah (often called Second Isaiah) are recognized as having been written in the period of the Exile, 587–538 B.C.E., after the fall of Jerusalem to the Babylonians and the deportation of many of the leaders and leading citizens of Jerusalem to Babylon.

The reasoning for such dating includes the radical difference in style from the Isaiah of the eighth century Jerusalem, the different content of these prophetic words, and the historical references given in the text itself. These passages are part of the book of Isaiah, and they do continue some of the major emphases of Isaiah of Jerusalem: God's interest in the people and divine care for them, God's sovereignty over history, and God's exalted holiness.

These chapters contain what many people assess to be the best poetry in the Bible. The verses here abound with vivid images from various aspects of human experience and Israel's historic past. One can see that the prophet uses every effort of rhetoric and persuasion to convince the fellow exiles of the message that burned in his mind.

The distinctive message of this prophet is that God will bring an end to the Exile that the people had been suffering for many decades. God will bring the people back to their beloved city of Jerusalem. The opening words announce that the people have suffered long enough for their past sins, and now God will free them from the deportation that had been accomplished by the Babylonians.

Certain theological themes are striking about the way this unnamed-to-us prophet conveys and enhances the basic message. Earlier prophets did not focus on God as creator to nearly the same degree as this one. God created the world, and thus shows mastery over all that is in the world. God can therefore be trusted when his message, conveyed by the prophet, is one of freedom to return home and serve God in the way they should desire.

God, moreover, is Lord of history. God had shown his divinity by liberating the Israelites when they were in bondage in Egypt. God will do the same now for the exiles in Babylon. God has not only done these wonderful works in the past but he had predicted that he would do them. He did them with power. Thus, God can be trusted now.

Second Isaiah was the first of the biblical authors to state explicitly that there exists only one God. Until his time, the biblical texts speak of the other gods with some seemingly implicit allowance for their existence. Second Isaiah tells the people outright that no other God exists beside the God who created the world, who freed the Israelites from the Egyptians, and who will deliver the exiles from the Babylonians.

Thus, this prophet has a theme of redemption, of restoring the people back to a condition that they had lost. This redemption is spoken of in various ways. Second Isaiah also speaks of a mysterious figure, identified as the Servant of the Lord. Four passages have been separated as the Songs of the Servant: 42:1–4; 49:1–6; 50:4–11; and 52:13–53:12. Various speakers are heard in these songs. The last song tells of the extreme suffering the servant undergoes before dying. His suffering is described as "for our transgressions"; and the song declares "the Lord laid on him the iniquity of us all." There have been many proposals about the identity of this figure. Believers see more than the immediate context. The Jewish tradition often sees the servant as the people Israel. The Christian tradition sees him as Jesus.

Distinctive too about Second Isaiah is the comparison of God to a woman, a mother: Isaiah 42:14; 45:10; 49:10 (and later 66:13). This feminine imagery for God appears only occasionally in the Bible. Second Isaiah has the greatest concentration of such depictions.

—Dr. John J. Schmitt

5
The Gospel of Mark

WHAT IS A "GOSPEL?"

The four Gospels ("good news"), the heart of the New Testament, are fundamental faith-witnesses of the apostolic church to God's final, definitive and all-transforming salvation of humankind in the person, words and actions of Jesus Christ, especially in his passion, death, and resurrection.

CRITICAL METHODS OF INTERPRETATION

Through the last two centuries scholars have developed "Historical-Critical Methods" for determining in a given Gospel the oral and literary sources from which it was compiled (Source Criticism); the types of discourse represented in the text (Form Criticism); and the unitary theological vision of the final editor, the evangelist (Redaction Criticism). In the process they have identified evidence of three stages in Gospel development: (1) words spoken and deeds performed by Jesus himself; (2) elements characteristic of an oral tradition of those

Raphel—"Transfiguration" Vatican Musuem
© Scala/Firenze

words and deeds; and (3) embellishments consistent with a unique overall vision, that of each evangelist as final redactor. New Testament exegetes also attempt to isolate the social and religious ambiance and challenges—the *Sitz-im-Leben* (life settings)—at work in each of these three stages: from those of Jesus's own lifetime to the situation of each evangelist's local church, hoping to discover a Gospel's fuller meaning from how it might have been created in response to those respective environments.

MARK, A SYNOPTIC SOURCE

Matthew, Mark and Luke are known as the "Synoptic Gospels" (Greek: *syn-op-*=see together) because they share many of the same stories about Jesus. This is true because Matthew and Luke both contain almost all of Mark. At the same time, because Matthew and Luke do not individually share material with Mark that is not found in the other, Mark seems to have pre-existed Matthew and Luke as one of their sources. Furthermore, because Matthew and Luke share material in common with each other not found in Mark—mostly sayings of Jesus, and material in the same sequence, most experts conclude that Matthew and Luke must have shared a second, unknown source as well, "Q" (German: *Quelle*=source). Mark, then, according to this so-called "Two-Source Theory," functioned as one of the two major sources for both Matthew and Luke.

MARK, INTERPRETER OF PETER?

Patristic writers (church authors from the late second to the seventh or eighth century) teach that Mark was written by an interpreter of St. Peter at Rome. Most scholars today agree to a Roman origin, suggesting further that Mark was written (a) between A.D. 65 and 70, and (b) for a predominantly Gentile Christian community (c) possibly threatened by, or in the midst of, a persecution, (d) a community which needed a greater understanding of the theology of the cross, and (e) which was expecting the imminent return of Christ (c. 13).

MESSIANIC SECRET?

In Mark's early chapters Jesus asks that his identity as Messiah not be publicized, a phenomenon long referred to (1901) as the "Messianic Secret." Some scholars suggest that this is a Markan literary device to lead readers, through the eyes of the disciples in the story, to discover how Jesus is an unexpected kind of Messiah, the Son of God whose mission is accomplished only though suffering and death. And this discovery, with its implications for Christian life, is something each Christian is faced with directly at the very center of the Gospel: "And who do *you* say that I am?" (8:29).

WHY THE STRANGE ENDING
TO MARK'S GOSPEL?

Scholars consider 16:9–20 a non- Markan addition because of its different style, vocabulary, and theology. Some argue that 16:8 is the author's intended ending; others that, since the Gospel would not have ended at 16:8 with the word, "*gar,*" meaning "for," the original ending must be lost. However, such an ending could be a clever way for the editor to signal his readers how the story is in fact not ended, that by his resurrection Jesus lives on and continues his saving activity in the life of the church. That also would be why the story centers on the Caesarea-Philippi question: "Who do *you* say that I am?" In other words, Jesus, alive in the church, inspiring it to gospel faith, continues to speak through that faith and therefore through *this* Gospel story whenever it is proclaimed in the church's liturgical assembly, directly calling each within its hearing to a personal discipleship of himself as their risen Lord.

THE WORD OF GOD, JESUS CHRIST, IN THE WORDS OF SCRIPTURE

The Gospel of Mark like all the Gospels, then, is ultimately the word of Christ in the church's words of faith in Christ. For Revelation itself is not primarily a book—the Bible with its Old and New Testaments—but a Person, Jesus Christ, the Word of God become human. Consequently, God's word sent to prophets and evangelists enshrined in the corpus of the Old and New Testaments is Christ, for God has no other word. The Bible is as it were an incarnation of the Word in the letter, which prepares and proclaims the one Incarnation, so that the whole Old Testament must be looked on as a prophecy of Christ. But this is possible only "when Jesus reads it to his church" (Origen) as he did to the disciples at Emmaus (Luke 24), showing them that the Bible speaks of himself.

CHRISTIAN FAITH AS PARTICIPATION IN THE FAITH OF CHRIST

If the Gospel of Mark is a witness of Christ speaking through the faith of the church, the textbook's selection to follow Mark, St. Paul's Letter to the Galatians, highlights how faith is the essence of Christian life. And the subsequent selection, I Corinthians 10–15, together with the Letter to the Hebrews found toward the end of the New Testament, teaches why this is so: because Christian faith is actually—through Christ's indwelling the church and each Christian (I Corinthians 12)—a participation in Christ's own faith in God during his human life on earth, that is, his obedience through suffering and darkness even unto death, making him the source of life to all who obey and serve him in that same faith (Hebrews 5:8–9; 12:2).

—*Rev. John D. Laurance, S.J.*

6

Galatians

1. PAUL'S WRITINGS

The apostle Paul is the only individual of the New Testament era
from whom we have original, personal writings. In terms of New Testament literature, Paul is clearly the most influential apostolic figure.
He is responsible for thirteen of the New Testament letters, although
many scholars think that only seven of these (Romans, 1 and 2
Corinthians, Galatians, Philippians, 1 Thessalonians and Philemon)
were written by Paul himself. The others (Ephesians, Colossians, 2
Thessalonians and the Pastoral Epistles: 1 Timothy, 2 Timothy and
Titus) are often called the pseudo-Paulines and may have been written by disciples of the apostle, following his death, in order to carry
on his literary and theological tradition. Paul's personal writings are
also the earliest literature which we possess from the Christian
movement. Paul wrote letters to his fledgling churches during the
late forties and throughout the fifties of the first century, and so his
writings antedate our written gospels by several decades. 1 Thessalonians is often thought to be his earliest letter, written in about 48

C.E. Again, because of their antiquity, Paul's writings are of unparalleled importance for understanding early Christianity's history and theology.

2. PAUL'S LIFE

The most reliable information for writing a biography of Paul comes from the letters he himself wrote, and much of this kind of information can be drawn from the Epistle to the Galatians. Paul was a Jew born in the Hellenized atmosphere of the *diaspora* at the very beginning of the Common Era. He was educated as a Pharisee, that is, an expert teacher and interpreter of the Jewish scriptures. He was also well educated in Greek grammar, rhetoric and philosophy, spoke Greek as his everyday language and used the Greek translation of the Old Testament for purposes of study, although he probably also knew Hebrew.

Paul was not a disciple of the earthly Jesus and was, in fact, personally involved in the discipline of early Christian believers as heretical to Judaism. In approximately 35 or 36 C.E. Paul had a visionary experience, a revelation, as a result of which he came to accept Jesus as Messiah and Son of God and felt himself called to be an apostle (a Christian missionary preacher) to the Gentiles in particular. He became associated with an established missionary effort toward the Gentiles, and went on numerous journeys through Greece and Asia Minor.

During his career as an apostle, Paul had contact with those who had followed Jesus during his earthly career and who were leaders of the mission to the Jews of the older Christian community in Jerusalem. He came to share a great deal of tradition about Jesus with those who had known him during his earthly life. Paul mentions his encounters with Peter, James and John especially. However, Paul also had some serious disagreements with these individuals, as Galatians 2 shows.

On his missionary journeys Paul worked as a craftsman to support himself, preaching in synagogues and in work places, gradually gathering converts. He remained in a city or town long enough to establish a viable community with local leadership, and then he moved on. Often his new churches had questions and insecurities about their new beliefs and community life. Sometimes other Christian missionaries, bringing different versions of the new Christian story, would enter these Pauline churches, causing great confusion and distress. Paul kept in contact with his churches by writing letters, which served as a vehicle for his presence and his teaching, answering their questions, admonishing, warning, correcting, and comforting them.

At the end of his life Paul collected a sum of money from his Gentile churches for the support of the Jewish Christians in Jerusalem. This "collection" expressed the unity of Jews and Gentiles as believers. However, it is uncertain whether this collection was accepted, since this unity was disputed at the time. Paul was probably arrested in Jerusalem, and he may have been taken to Rome. He probably died a martyr in approximately A.D. 60. We have no certain knowledge of the time and manner of his death.

---

3. THE EPISTLE

The Epistle to the Galatians was written during the 50's of the Common Era to a church founded by Paul, but ready to accept "another gospel" preached by other missionaries who arrived after Paul had left. While Paul's gospel emphasized faith in the death of Christ for our sins and in his resurrection, the "different" gospel added circumcision and observance of the law of Moses to faith in Jesus Christ.

The Galatian Christians were converted by Paul from paganism. They had not previously been observant Jews. However, they were impressed with the authority and knowledge of the newly arrived Jewish missionaries. Their message and status challenged Paul's authority over the Galatian community. In response to their challenge and the Galatian rejection of Paul and his gospel, Paul must himself present a strong scriptural argument in support of his understanding of salvation in Jesus Christ from those same Jewish scriptures. For this reason, the Epistle to the Galatians is especially useful for appreciating the continuities and contrasts between Judaism and Christianity or between the Old and New Testaments. It was Paul's intention to explain that very thing to his confused converts.

—*Dr. Carol L. Stockhausen*

7

1 Corinthians 10–15

During his missionary travels, Paul had founded the Christian community at Corinth. Subsequently, through oral reports and in a letter sent him by the community, he became aware of problems there. 1 Corinthians consists of responses to the reports and letter. The problems Paul addresses reflect at root a selfish individualism or factiousness in the community. Many of the Corinthian Christians believe that all that is important is to "know" the fact of their salvation, and that this knowledge in fact liberates them from duties of love to their fellow Christians or even to Christ.

Paul therefore begins his letter by reminding the Corinthians of the message he preached to them. This message was the message of the Cross. Contrary to all worldly wisdom and all expectations, God's power is manifested in Christ's humbling of himself and finally accepting his death. Christians must imitate Christ in living not for themselves but for their fellow Christians—together, Christ's Body. The supreme gift of the Holy Spirit to Christians is therefore love, loving service and self-sacrifice to Christ's Body. Paul's own work as an apostle exemplifies such love, and his authority is exercised through a call to the Corinthians to imitate him in imitating Christ.

(This last point is developed further in 2 Corinthians in response to more explicit challenges among the Corinthians to Paul's authority).

These principles are applied to the specifics of the Corinthian problems. Major points from your reading are as follows:

(1) **Meat from pagan sacrifices (ch. 10).** Just as the Israelites in the desert on the Exodus from Egypt were punished for their lack of fidelity, even as they were being saved ("baptized . . . in the cloud and sea") and nourished with "supernatural food and drink" (10:3–4), so will the Corinthians be punished if they are not faithful to Christ who nourishes them in the Eucharist.

(2) **The Eucharist and Christian life (11:17–34).** The Eucharist is a proclamation of Christ's death, by which he gave himself up for us to establish a covenant relationship with us. To receive it in a context of selfishness and division is to reject the Christ who offers himself in it, with the result of condemnation rather than blessing.

(3) **Spiritual gifts and love (ch. 12–14).** The work of the Spirit is to affirm Jesus Christ. Spiritual gifts such as wisdom, knowledge, faith, healing, miracles, prophecy, discernment of spirits, praying in tongues and their interpretation (12:8–10) manifest God's presence and power and love and are not given for self-aggrandizement but for the good of the entire Body of Christ. The greatest such gift is therefore love.

(4) **The resurrection (ch. 15).** The Corinthians already believe that Christ is risen—this was the faith Paul received and passed on to them; if it is not true, their faith is in vain and they who have lived and died for Christ are pitiable. But if Christ is risen, then the members of his Body will also rise. In response to skepticism about bodily resurrection, Paul insists that resurrection is not mere resuscitation of a corpse but will change their corruptible (mortal) bodies into an incorruptible (immortal) form, as different from their present bodies as a plant is from its seed. Their

transformation, not yet complete, can only be completed after death or when Christ returns at the end of time if they subject themselves to the Father in Christ.

—*Rev. William S. Kurz, S. J.*

II
Readings from
Christian Tradition

*"Jesus came forward and addressed
[the eleven] in these words:
'Full authority has been given to me
both in heaven and on earth:
Go, therefore, and make disciples
of all nations. Baptize them in the name
of the Father, and of the Son,
and of the Holy Spirit.
Teach them to carry out everything
I have commanded you.
And know that I am with you always,
until the end of the world!'"*

Matthew 28: 18–20

8

The First Apology
(A.D.148–161)

ST. JUSTIN MARTYR (†165)
(SELECTIONS)

INTRODUCTION

This selection from *The First Apology* of St. Justin Martyr belongs to
the post-apostolic period in church history between the death of the
last apostle, St. John the Evangelist (ca. A.D. 96?), and the so-called
"Patristic Age" which began with the first "Father of the Church," St.
Irenaeus (ca.185). That later era lasted through St. Isidore of Seville
(†636) in the West, and St. John Damascene (†749) in the East, followed then by the Middle Ages or Medieval period.

A philosopher and Christian Apologist, Justin (ca. 100–165) was
born of non-Christian parents at Flavia Neopolis (ancient Shechem,
modern Nablus) in Samaria. In his search for truth, he investigated
the teachings, first of the Stoics, then of the Peripatetics and finally
the Pythagoreans before encountering an old man by the seashore
who revealed to him the wisdom of Christianity (ca. 130). After his

baptism Justin became a teacher of Christianity at Ephesus and then moved on to Rome where he founded a school. He arrived there during the reign of Emperor Antoninus Pius (138–161). It was probably during the prefecture of Junius Rusticus (163–167) that he refused to offer sacrifice to the Roman gods, and so was scourged and beheaded for the faith.

"Apology" here means "explanation," specifically an explanation, directed to non-Christians in authority, of the reasonableness of the Christian faith, and of the probity and good citizenship of Christians. In chapters 65–67 of his *First Apology* St. Justin gives an account of how the eucharistic liturgy of his time took place: with continuous readings (*lectio continua*) from Scripture, prayers of the faithful, and the presider's spontaneous rendering, according to a traditional pattern, of the eucharistic prayer. Justin also supplies his own theological understanding of Christ's real presence in the bread and wine of the Eucharist, and he teaches how the liturgy carries with it ethical demands for everyday Christian life.

In addition to its being a thanksgiving to the Father for salvation in Christ, the Eucharist has always been understood as a commitment to, and an empowerment in Christ for, a life of sacrificial love of God and neighbor. This connection between liturgy and life[1] is evidenced in a document contemporary with Justin's, *The Martyrdom of Polycarp* (ca. A.D. 155), where St. Polycarp of Smyrna in Asia Minor just before his martyrdom by fire prays in language ("*I give you thanks that you have counted me worthy . . . [to] . . . have a part in the number of your martyrs*") similar to the liturgical language used both by Justin ("*. . . for our being counted worthy to receive everything from him*"), and by Hippolytus in *The Apostolic Tradition* eucharistic prayer ("*. . . giving*

---

[1] For a helpful theological explanation of this relationship, see Karl Rahner, "How to Receive a Sacrament and Mean It," *Theology Digest* 19:3 (Autumn 1971) 227–234 (a digest of: *Theological Investigations* 14 [NY: Seabury, 1976]161–184).

you thanks that you have held us worthy to stand before you and give you priestly worship”), the next selection in this book.

–Rev. John D. Laurance, S.J.

TEXT

Chapter 1—Address

To the Emperor Titus Ælius Adrianus Antoninus Pius Augustus Caesar, and to his son Verissimus the Philosopher, and to Lucius the Philosopher, the natural son of Caesar, and the adopted son of Pius, a lover of learning, and to the sacred Senate, with the whole People of the Romans, I, Justin, the son of Priscus and grandson of Bacchius, natives of Flavia Neapolis in Palestine, present this address and petition in behalf of those of all nations who are unjustly hated and wantonly abused—myself among them.

* * *

Chapter 65—Sacraments of Initiation

After washing the one who believes and having joined him to our ranks, we then lead him to those who are called “brothers” to where they are assembled, in order to make communal prayers for ourselves and for the enlightened (baptized) one, and for all others everywhere, that through our works we may be counted worthy, now that we have learned the truth, to be considered good citizens and guardians of the commandments—that thus we be saved with an everlasting salvation. After ending the prayers, we welcome one another with a kiss. There is then brought to the one who presides over the brothers bread and a cup of water and of mixed wine; and taking them, he sends up praise and glory to the Father of the universe through the name of the Son and of the Holy Spirit, and he makes a prolonged eucharist for our being counted worthy to receive everything from him. And when he has concluded the prayers and the eucharist, all the people present agree by saying “Amen.” This word Amen in the Hebrew language signifies the *Genoito* (Greek: “Let it be so”). After the presider has

5

10

15

20

25 made eucharist and all the people agreed, those whom we call "deacons" distribute to all present a sharing in the eucharisted bread and
wine and water, and they carry [it] to those who are absent.

Chapter 66—Christ's Real Presence

And we call the food itself Eucharist, of which no one is allowed to
partake except the one believing that what we teach is true—one who
30 has been washed with the washing for remission of sins and regener-
ation, and who is living as Christ taught. For we do not take these to
be ordinary bread and ordinary drink; but just as Jesus Christ our
Savior, who was made flesh through the Word of God, possessed flesh
and blood for our salvation, so likewise have we been taught that the
35 food which has been eucharisted by the prayer of his word—and from
which by metabolism our own blood and flesh are nourished—is the
flesh and blood of that Jesus who we have been taught was made
flesh. For the apostles, in the memoirs they composed called Gospels,
handed on to us what they were taught in the same way (1 Cor
40 11:23): that Jesus took bread and, when he made the eucharist, said,
"Do this in remembrance of me, this is my body;" and that, in the
same way, having taken the cup and made the eucharist, he said,
"This is my blood;" and to them alone did he give it. The wicked
devils in the mysteries of Mithras have taught people to imitate this.
45 For as you either know or have to power of finding out, in their mystic rites of initiation bread and a cup of water are set forth with
certain incantations.

Chapter 67—The Sunday Eucharist

Now after all this is over, we continually remind each other of these
things. And those who are well provided for come to the aid of all the
50 needy; and we are always present to each other. Over everything that
we offer we bless the Maker of all things through his Son Jesus Christ,
and through the Holy Spirit. And on the day named after the sun,
there is a gathering of all who live in cities or in the country into one
place, and the memoirs of the apostles or the writings of the prophets

Mosaic of Abel and Melchisedek Offering Sacrifices, from San Vitale Church in
Ravenna, Italy.
© Scala/Firenze

are read as long as there is time; then, when the reader stops, the   55
presider makes a verbal exhortation that we imitate all these beautiful
things. Then we all stand up together and send forth prayers; and, as
we said before, after we stop our prayers, bread and wine and water
are brought forward, and the presider sends up prayers and makes
eucharists in the same way, as much as he is able to do, and the peo-   60
ple assent, saying the Amen; and there is a distribution and
participation in what has been eucharisted, and through the deacons
some is sent to those absent. And they who are well off and willing
give what each in his own judgment decides, and what is collected is
set by the presider, and he gives aid to orphans and widows and those   65
who have need because of sickness or some other reason, and to those
in chains and strangers passing among us—simply put, [the presider]
cares for all who are wanting. Indeed, we all assemble together on the
day of the sun, because it is the first day, the day on which God
changed darkness and matter and made the ordered world; and Jesus   70
Christ our Savior rose from the dead on this same day. For they cru-

cified him on the day before the day of Kronos (Saturn); and on the day after the day of Kronos, which is the day of the sun, in his appearance to his apostles and disciples he taught them all that I have entrusted to your consideration.

75

9

The Apostolic Tradition, 4
(ca. A.D. 215?)

ST. HIPPOLYTUS OF ROME
(CA. 170–CA. 236)

INTRODUCTION

The so-called *Apostolic Tradition* (AT), originally written in Greek, is an example of a "church order," that is, a book of instructions on how to run a local church. Other such "church orders" include *The Didache* (ca. AD. 100), *The Didascalia Apostolorum* (ca. A.D. 235) and *The Apostolic Constitutions* (ca. A.D. 385). The AT has traditionally borne the name of St. Hippolytus of Rome, a highly influential presbyter and theologian of the Church at Rome, as its final redactor. In very recent years this assignation has come under serious attack. Although much of the text dates from the third if not the second century, it seems to have been modified in later centuries, and its Roman provenance is anything but certain.

41

The 43 chapters of the AT were actually lost to the church for more than 1,000 years, reappearing only when a Bohairic translation of it was published in 1848. Then it was known simply as "The Egyptian Church Order." Later in the nineteenth century Sahidic Coptic, Arabic, Ethiopic and Latin manuscript versions of the work were also discovered. In 1906 E. von der Goltz suggested that this treatise was in fact the lost AT of Hippolytus. Studies by W. Schwartz in 1910 and R. H. Connolly in 1916 agreed with his theory. Finally, critical editions of the work were produced, first in 1937 by the Anglican Benedictine liturgical scholar, Dom Gregory Dix, and then in 1946 (Paris) and 1962 (Münster) by the Belgian, Dom Bernard Botte, O.S.B.

In addition to providing ordination prayers and a eucharistic prayer, the AT also gives directions on the proper recognition and/or installation of confessors, virgins, widows, readers, and subdeacons in the Church. Next it deals with baptism, beginning with a list of professions one must renounce before becoming a Christian, such as actor and brothel-keeper. Finally, the AT sets down norms for daily prayer and other aspects of good, ordered Christian living.

The AT eucharistic prayer below begins with an allusion to The Letter to the Hebrews 1:1, as does Vatican II's "Constitution on the Sacred Liturgy" (par. 5), found at the end of this volume. Both rely heavily on the theology of The Letter to the Hebrews, seeing the eucharistic liturgy as the Church's being taken up into God's saving self-revelation in Christ by the work of the Holy Spirit and through its thanksgiving-memorial of Christ's own once-and-for-all victorious faith-obedience. With the post-Vatican II Catholic reforms a new "Eucharistic Prayer II" was created, modeled on this early Christian prayer. Subsequently, Lutheran, Episcopalian and other church denominations fashioned eucharistic prayers also based on this same AT prototype. Three are set side-by-side to the original on the pages that follow. Note how each twentieth-century prayer reflects the particular faith emphases of the denomination it represents.

—Rev. John D. Laurance, S.J.

THE APOSTOLIC TRADITION, 4 (ca. A.·D. 215?)

43

APOSTOLIC TRADITION
Chapter 4

P. The Lord be with you.

R. And with your spirit.

P. Lift up your hearts.

R. We have lifted them to the Lord.

P. Let us give thanks to the Lord.

R. It is proper and right.

P. We give you thanks, O God, through your beloved son Jesus Christ, whom in these end times you sent as our savior and redeemer and the messenger of your will. He is your inseparable Word through whom you made all things and who is well-pleasing to you. You sent him from heaven into the motherhood of a virgin and, made flesh, he became manifest as your Son, born of the Holy Spirit and the Virgin. Doing your will and creating for you a holy people, he extended his hands in suffering in order to release those who trust in you. When he was betrayed into his voluntary Passion—in order to dissolve death, break the chains of the devil, trample down hell, destroy its power, lead the just into the light, and typify the resurrection—, taking bread and giving thanks, he said, "Take, eat, this is my body which is broken for you." In the same way with the chalice, "This is my blood which is poured out for you. When you do this, do it as my memorial."

Remembering, therefore, his death and resurrection, we offer you this bread and chalice, giving you thanks that you have held us worthy to stand before you and give you priestly worship. And we ask you to send your Holy Spirit on the offering of your holy church. In gathering them together, let all who participate in these sacred mysteries be filled with your Holy Spirit, in order to affirm their faith in the Truth, that we might praise and glorify you through your son Jesus Christ, through whom be glory and honor to you with the Holy Spirit in your holy church both now and forever. *Amen.*

MISSAL OF PAUL VI
Eucharistic Prayer II

The Lord be with you. . .(etc.)

Father, it is our duty and our salvation always and everywhere to give you thanks through your beloved Son, Jesus Christ. He is the Word through whom you made the universe, the Savior you sent to redeem us. By the power of the Holy Spirit he took flesh and was born of the Virgin Mary. For our sake he opened his arms on the cross; he put an end to death and revealed the resurrection. In this he fulfilled your will and won for you a holy people. And so we join the angels and the saints in proclaiming your glory as we say:

Holy, holy, holy Lord, God of power and might, heaven and earth are full of your glory. Hosanna in the highest. Blessed is he who comes in the name of the Lord. Hosanna in the highest.

Lord, you are holy indeed, the fountain of all holiness. Let your Spirit come upon these gifts to make them holy, so that they may become for us the body and blood of our Lord, Jesus Christ. Before he was given up to death, a death he freely accepted, he took bread and gave you thanks. He broke the bread, gave it to his disciples, and said: **Take this, all of you, and eat it: this is my body which will be given up for you**. When supper was ended, he took the cup. Again he gave you thanks and praise, gave the cup to his disciples, and said: **Take this, all of you, and drink from it: this is the cup of my blood, the blood of the new and everlasting covenant. It will be shed for you and for all so that sins may be forgiven. Do this in memory of me.** Let us proclaim the Mystery of Faith:

Christ has died, Christ has risen, Christ will come again.

In memory of his death and resurrection, we offer you, Father, this life-giving bread, this saving cup. We thank you for counting us worthy to stand in your presence and serve you. May all of us who share in the body and blood of Christ be brought together in unity by the Holy Spirit. Lord, remember your Church throughout the world;

THE APOSTOLIC TRADITION, 4 (ca. A.D. 215?)

45

make us grow in love, together with _____ our Pope, and _____ our bishop, and all the clergy. Remember our brothers and sisters who have gone to their rest in the hope of rising again; bring them and all the departed into the light of your presence. Have mercy on us all; make us worthy to share eternal life with Mary, the virgin Mother of God, with the apostles, and with all the saints who have done your will throughout the ages. May we praise you in union with them, and give you glory through your Son, Jesus Christ. Through him, with him, and in him, in the unity of the Holy Spirit, all glory and honor is yours, almighty Father, forever and ever. *Amen.*

EUCHARISTIC PRAYER IV

(Lutheran)

The Lord be with you . . . (etc.)

It is indeed right and salutary that we should at all times and in all places offer thanks and praise to you, O Lord, holy Father, through Christ our Lord; who on this day overcame death and the grave, and by his glorious resurrection opened to us the way of everlasting life. And so, with the Church on earth and the hosts of heaven, we praise your name and join their unending hymn:

Holy, holy, holy, Lord, God of power and might: Heaven and earth are full of your glory. Hosanna in the highest. Blessed is he who comes in the name of the Lord. Hosanna in the highest.

We give you thanks, Father, through Jesus Christ, your beloved Son, whom you sent in this end of the ages to save and redeem us and to proclaim to us your will. He is your Word, inseparable from you. Through him you created all things, and in him you take delight. He is your Word, sent from heaven to a virgin's womb. He there took on our nature and our lot and was shown forth as your Son, born of the Holy Spirit and of the virgin Mary. It is he, our Lord Jesus, who fulfilled all your will and won for you a holy people; he stretched out his hands in suffering in order to free from suffering those who trust you. It is he who, handed over to a death he freely accepted, in order to destroy death, to break the bonds of the evil one, to crush hell underfoot, to give light to the righteous, to establish his covenant, and to show forth the resurrection, taking bread and giving thanks to you, said: Take and eat; this is my body, broken for you. Do this for the remembrance of me. In the same way he took the cup, gave thanks, and gave it for all to drink, saying: This is my blood poured out for you. Do this for the remembrance of me.

Remembering, then, his death and resurrection, we lift this bread and cup before you, giving you thanks that you have made us worthy to stand before you and to serve you as your priestly people. And we ask you: Send your Spirit upon these gifts of your Church; gather into one all who share this bread and wine; fill us with your Holy Spirit to establish our faith in truth, that we may praise and glorify you through your Son Jesus Christ. Through him all glory and honor are yours, Almighty Father, with the Holy Spirit, in your holy Church both now and forever. *Amen.*

COMMUNION PRAYER
(The Reformed Church in America)

The Lord be with you . . . (etc.)

Holy and right it is, and our joyful duty to give thanks to you at all times and in all places, O Lord our Creator, almighty and everlasting God! You created heaven with all its hosts and the earth with all its plenty. You have given us life and being and preserve us by your providence. But you have shown us the fullness of your love in sending into the world your Son, Jesus Christ, the eternal Word, made flesh for us and for our salvation. For the precious gift of this mighty Savior who has reconciled us to you we praise and bless you, O God.

THE APOSTOLIC TRADITION, 4 (ca. A.D. 215?)

47

With your whole Church on earth and with all the company of heaven we worship and adore your glorious name.

Holy, holy, holy, Lord, God of hosts! Heaven and earth are full of your glory. Hosanna in the highest! Blessed is he that comes in the name of the Lord. Hosanna in the highest! (*A brief period of silence.*)

Most righteous God, we remember in this Supper the perfect sacrifice offered once on the cross by our Lord Jesus Christ for the sin of the whole world. In the joy of his resurrection and in expectation of his coming again, we offer ourselves to you as holy and living sacrifices.

Together we proclaim the mystery of the faith: *Christ has died! Christ is risen! Christ will come again!*

Send your Holy Spirit upon us, we pray, that the bread which we break and the cup which we bless may be to us the communion of the body and blood of Christ. Grant that, being joined together in him, we may attain to the unity of the faith and grow up in all things into Christ our Lord. And as this grain has been gathered from many fields into one loaf, and these grapes from many fields into one cup, grant, O Lord, that your whole Church may soon be gathered from the ends of the earth into your kingdom. Even so, come, Lord Jesus!

COMMUNION

The Lord Jesus, the same night he was betrayed, took bread; and when he had given thanks, he broke it and gave it to them, saying, "Take, eat; this is my body which is broken for you: do this in remembrance of me." After the same manner also, he took the cup when they had supped, saying, "This cup is the new testament in my blood; this do, as often as you drink it, in remembrance of me."

(*In partaking of the bread it shall be said:*) The bread which we break is the communion of the body of Christ.

(*In partaking of the cup it shall be said:*) The cup of blessing which we bless is the communion of the body of Christ.

10

Nicene–Constantinopolitan Creed

COUNCIL OF CONSTANTINOPLE 1 (381)

INTRODUCTION

Origins

Properly called the creed of the Council of Constantinople, 381, this document is also known as the "Nicene-Constantinopolitan" creed because its roots, particularly in terms of its theology, go back to a council held in Nicaea (a town outside Constantinople, now present-day Istanbul). Since 381 this creed has functioned as the fundamental expression of Christian belief. It is recited, e.g., in the Roman Catholic Mass, in the Lutheran Service, as well as in the services of most mainstream Christian denominations.[1]

---

[1] Some Free Church denominations have the creed printed in hymnals, but, it must be admitted, some Free Churches do not use the creed at all.

As a statement of the fundamental beliefs shared by most Christians, the Nicene-Constantinopolitan creed has played an important role in the modern Christian ecumenical movement. The creed has also functioned within each denomination that recites it as a document of self-definition, similar to the role the Constitution plays in American self-definition: 'This is who we are, what we believe, what keeps us who we are, what we test new developments against.'

Purpose of Creeds

"Creeds" in general perhaps originate with the very first generation of the Church as summaries of Christian beliefs. Such summaries functioned as teaching devices for new Christians: "This is what we believe, and to join our community you too must believe this." Or: "There's a lot of stuff to learn about, but this is what you really have to believe!" We know that by the middle of the second century Christian communities used such creedal summaries as part of baptism. The candidate for admission into the Church was asked a series of questions on their grasp of the faith, such as, "Do you believe in God the creator," to which the candidate was expected to answer, "Yes, I believe." Such statements of the faith were also used to test out claims to authority. If an argument was made by someone that some book was inspired and should be treated as "Scripture," then the content of the book was tested against the creed to see if it really was inspired and represented the beliefs of the community. Agreement wasn't necessary on a word for word basis, but the basic understanding expressed in the community's creed was the rule.

Typical Structure

Such creeds often followed a narrative or story form, usually divided into four "episodes" or "acts": (1) God, usually called the "Father" and always recognized as the creator; (2) the Son of God, who comes from (in both senses of that phrase) God the Father, and who comes to save us; (3) the Holy Spirit, who is very much associated with the origins

Abrahamic typology of Christ's sacrifice and God as three persons, San Vitale, Ravenna.
© Scala/Art Resource, NY

and sustaining energy of the Church; and (4) an assortment of plot lines or details that further identify the believing community or the fate of that community. The core story of each of these episodes is developed in varying detail, but plot line number two, the Son, usually gets the most attention and development in the form of a summary of the key highlights from the life of Christ.

Historical Background

Whenever any of the four episodes of the creed are developed in any detail, that is because someone else is denying that particular element. For example, almost all the creeds that date from after the New Testament describe God as the maker of heaven and earth because there were people who believed that heaven and earth come not from God, but from some evil source. Similarly, creeds emphasize the reality of Jesus' birth from Mary because some people taught that Jesus wasn't really human (He was "better" than that!).

In the fourth century there was a major disagreement over whether the Son was "God" the way the Father was "God". The argument began around A.D. 318, when a priest named Arius taught that only God the Father was really "God" because only he was eternal and uncaused. The Son was not eternal because he was caused, and so he was not "God" in the full sense of the term. He was, in fact, a very special kind of creature. Not quite God, but God enough for us. Arius' bishop, Alexander, the bishop of Alexandria, Egypt, and Alexander's successor, Athanasius (a lot of *a*-word names here!) opposed Arius, and in 325, in Nicaea, a town outside the Emperor's new city, Constantinople, a group of bishops gathered from across the Greek-speaking part of the Empire to judge Arius' theology. The overwhelming majority of those bishops gathered in Nicaea condemned Arius' theology and he and some of his sympathizers were sent into exile. The Council produced a creed which stated, in no uncertain terms, that the Son was God as the Father was God. The fact was expressed using language which can be translated as "essence" or "substance" or even "being." The Son had the same "essence" as the Father.

"Person" and "Substance"

Arius' tendency to see the Son as a kind of "God-Lite," as it were, was condemned, but the creed went so far in stating divine unity that it left unsaid how the Father and Son were really different, and not just two appearances of this real existence, "God". Did the Father and the Son have the same substance the way Robin Williams and Mrs. Doubtfire have the same substance?

You have probably been taught, or at least heard, that "Trinity" means that God is "one in nature or being" *and* "three persons." This is the insight that most Christians will come to by 381 and will be signaled by the creed of Constantinople, 381. But the problem was that there was, when the argument started, no clear understanding of what it meant to be an individual. Your second grade teacher may have told you we are each as different as the little paper snowflakes you cut out and taped to your classroom window, but exactly how we were each different took some figuring out. In the ancient world the difference between this or that person was basically the difference between this hunk of human flesh and that hunk of human flesh. Difference was physically-based. That kind of difference could not apply to God who wasn't physical, so how were the real differences in God to be understood? Figuring out a way to articulate what it means to be a different person without depending on a material understanding took a while, as did finding a balance between a belief in God's unity and a belief in the different persons who were God. This development took from 318 until 381 and then some.

Basically, some Christians figured that one way to express the basis of the difference between Father and Son was to focus on their relationship(s). Relationships identify us as persons, make us persons. In the case of Father and Son the titles reflect their defining relationships (who they are), but those titles also express the basis for their unity. A son or daughter has the same nature as a parent. The Creed of 381 also recognized that Holy Spirit was divine and a person, but the scriptural language (e.g., "Father," "Son") for recognizing the relationships was not as clear and helpful. Spirit? Breath? The Creed of 381 uses the term "proceeds" to name the causal relationship that identifies the Holy Spirit and which also serves as the basis for the Spirit's common divinity with the Father and Son. But the Council recognized that it wasn't as clear about how to understand that generative relationship, those "processions," and the distinct identity of the Holy Spirit. The language the creed uses of the Holy Spirit is not quite as confident as the language it uses of the Son.

The texts of early baptismal creeds and creeds of various Christian churches are available on the internet:

http://www.iclnet.org/pub/resources/text/history/creeds.Bible.txt

http://www.Bible.ca/indexchurches.htm

—*Dr. Michel R. Barnes*

TEXT

Council of Constantinople I 381

Ecumenical II (against the Macedonians, etc.)

Condemnation of the Heretics[2]

Can. 1. The faith of the three hundred and eighteen fathers who assembled at Nicea in Bithynia is not to be disregarded; but it remains authoritative, and all heresy is to be anathematized: and especially that of the Eunomians or of the Anomians, and that of the Arians, or
5   that of the Eudoxians, and that of the Macedonians, that is to say of those opposing the Spirit, and that of the Sabellians, of the Marcellians and that of the Photinians and that of the Apollinarians.

Can. 1. [Version of Dionysius Exiguus] The faith of three hundred and eighteen Fathers, who convened at Nicea in Bithynia, ought not
10   to be violated; but remains firm and stable. Every heresy ought to be anathematized, and especially those of the Eunomians or Anomians, and of the Arians or Eudoxians, and of the Macedonians or those who oppose the Holy Spirit, and of the Marcellians, and of the Photinians, and of the Apollinarians.

The "Nicene-Constantinopolitan"[3] Creed

15   We believe in one God, Father omnipotent, maker of heaven and earth, and of all things visible and invisible. And in one Lord Jesus

---

[2] Msi III gr. 557 E., lat. 566 D. Coll. Hfl II 14; Hrd I 809 A.

[3] ACOec II 1 P. 2, 80; Msi III 565 A; H 165 f.; Missale Romanum; Hrd I 813 B; ML 48, 772 A; Bar(Th)ad 381 n. 29 (5, 461b). Cf. Rev. d'hist. eccl. 32 (1936) 809 ff. (J. Lebon). See the text slightly changed of Theodorus Mops. in A. Rücker, *Ritus baptismi et Missae* . . ., Monasterii 1933, 42 f. This creed, after the Synods of EPHESUS and CHALCEDON, passed into the liturgical use of the Oriental Church, and this same thing took place in the West about the end of the eighth century through St. Paulinus of Aquileia against the Adoptianists. Those words which are enclosed in brackets show the liturgical text almost as it was prepared by St. Paulinus, *Rech. de théol. anc. et méd.* 1 [1929] 7 ff. (B. Capelle).

Christ, the only begotten Son of God, born of the Father before all ages, light of light, true God of true God, begotten not made, consubstantial with the Father, by whom all things were made, who for us men and for our salvation came down and was made flesh by the 20 Holy Spirit and of the Virgin Mary, and became man, and was crucified for us by Pontius Pilate, suffered, and was buried and arose again the third day, according to the Scripture, and ascended into heaven, and sits at the right hand of the Father, and is coming again with glory to judge the living and the dead; of whose kingdom there shall 25 be no end. And in the Holy Spirit, the Lord, the giver of life, who proceeds from the Father, who together with the Father and Son is worshipped and glorified, who spoke through the prophets. In one holy, Catholic, and Apostolic Church. We confess one baptism for the remission of sins. We look for the resurrection of the dead, and 30 the life of eternity to come. Amen.

[Version of Dionysius Exiguus]

We believe [I believe] in one God the Father almighty, maker of heaven and earth, and of all things visible and invisible. And in one Lord Jesus Christ, the Son of God, born of the Father [the only 35 begotten Son of God. And born of the Father] before all ages. [God of God, light of light] true God of true God. Born [Begotten], not made, consubstantial with the Father, by whom all things were made. Who for us men and for our salvation [and for our salvation] came down from heaven. And was incarnate by the Holy Spirit of the Vir- 40 gin Mary, and was made human [was made man]. And he was crucified [He was crucified also] for us under Pontius Pilate, [suffered]—and was buried. And on the third day he rose again, [according to the Scriptures. And] ascended into heaven, sits at the right hand of the Father, [and] will come again with glory to judge 45 the living and the dead; of whose kingdom there shall not be an end. And in the Holy Spirit, the Lord and giver of life, proceeding from

50   the Father, [who proceeds from the Father and the Son,[4] who] to be adored with the Father and the Son [is adored together with] and to be glorified together with (them) [and is glorified together with], who spoke through the holy Prophets [by the Prophets]. And in one holy Catholic and apostolic Church. We confess [I confess] one baptism for the remission of sins. We expect [And I expect] the resurrection of the dead, and the life of a future age [to come]. Amen.

---

[4] The addition "and the Son" was first made in Spain. From here this custom passed over into Gaul, then into Germany, as is clear from the Gallican liturgy of Moneius at the beginning of the fifth century, from the Synod of the Forum Julii 791, of Frankfurt 794, of Aquisgranum (Aachen), 809, which asked Leo III that it be reaccepted by the Roman Church. This, however, Leo refused, not because he rejected the dogma, but because he feared to add anything to the traditional form. Afterwards, indeed, when St. Henry obtained from Benedict VIII (1012–1024) his request that the creed be sung among the ceremonies of the Masses, the addition was accepted.

11

Confessions: Book Eight

AUGUSTINE OF HIPPO (354–430)

Augustine (354-430) must certainly have a place in any list of people who have shaped Christian belief in a fundamental way.

Spiritual Autobiography

One of the most important of Augustine's many contributions is his invention of a type of book: the spiritual or psychological autobiography. No Christian, before the *Confessions,* had ever written an account of her or his life. Books about other Christians' lives, holy people who could serve as role models, had begun to gain popularity at about the time Augustine was born. The most famous and influential was *The Life of Antony* by Athanasius, bishop of Alexandria, Egypt. Quickly translated from Greek into Latin, this work influenced many young Christians, including Augustine himself and his friends.

The *Confessions* was a new kind of book for two reasons: It was about the person writing, and there is no presumption that the author is "holy," although there is still the idea that the story of what happened to Augustine can help other Christians in their lives (precisely because so much of Augustine's life seemed so unholy).

Family Background

Augustine was born into a family with a non-Christian father and a very pious Christian mother. His mother, Monica, was to remain a strong influence throughout Augustine's life, in part because his father died when Augustine was a teenager, and in part because she was a very special person who had great hopes for her son. Despite his mom's strong belief, Augustine was not much of a believing Christian when he was young. Until he was almost thirty he experimented with different beliefs, having, as a teenager, decided that Christianity was basically a religion for stupid people.

Milan and Ambrose

By profession Augustine was a rhetorician, that is, someone basically who trains public figures–like politicians and lawyers–in speaking and debate. In the culture in which Augustine lived this job was more important than it sounds as though it would be in ours. In addition, he was good at what he did and, although just a young man from "the sticks" of North Africa, he got a job teaching in Rome. Rome was officially still the capital of the western half of the Roman Empire, but the Emperor himself lived in Milan, and the government (and government groupies) followed the Emperor there. Augustine himself moved to Milan, and it was in that city that he came across Ambrose, bishop of Milan, and a pretty bright guy himself. Ambrose was able to help Augustine through his difficulties with what seemed like the stupid parts of Christianity. What Augustine came to see was that the problem he experienced was not so much with Christianity, but with himself. Augustine had a problem, and what the *Confessions* turns out to be about is his discovery of the problem and the solution.

Theology of the Confessions

Augustine begins his life story with childhood memories of events illustrating that there is something in people that drives them, not simply to doing bad things, but to enjoying doing bad things. There doesn't seem to have been a sentimental bone in Augustine's body because his portraits of being a baby, a child and a teenager are anything but cute and sweet. Augustine was not an uncommonly evil person; he was just more honest than most people about those moments which most of us try very hard to forget, or at least to hide. He was particularly bothered, as a young man, by feelings of lust. If he were living today he would be called a "womanizer." However, Augustine was not wanton with these feelings. As a young man he had a mistress to whom he was completely faithful for years (until his mom broke up the relationship because it wasn't going to help his career).

Augustine's desires were, for him, a window on to the fact that something deep down inside of him was basically broken: he knew what was best for him, he knew what was the right thing to do, and yet so many of his choices set him up to do the wrong thing. Augustine's insight was that on our own, our innate moral strength is too broken to overcome our own tendency to fail, but with God's help, with God's "grace," we can overcome our moral weaknesses and do the right thing. Augustine's "conversion" was not so much an experience of the fact that we all need God's help as it was the experience of receiving God's help.

The full text of the *Confessions* is available on the internet:

http://www.ccel.org/a/augustine/confessions/confessions.html

—*Dr. Michel R. Barnes*

Church of St. Ambrose in Milan.
© Scala/Firenze

TEXT

Book Eight (Age 31)

Outline:

I

Let me, O my God, remember with thanks to Thee and confess Thy mercies upon me. Let my bones be pierced through with Thy love, and let them say: *Who is like unto Thee, O Lord, Thou hast broken my bonds, I will sacrifice to Thee the sacrifice of praise.* How Thou hast broken them I shall tell and all who adore Thee will say as they listen: 5
Blessed be the Lord in heaven and on earth, great and wonderful is His name.

Your words had rooted deep in my heart and I was fenced about on all sides by You. Of Your eternal life I was now certain, though I saw it *in a dark manner and as through a glass.* All my former doubt about an incorruptible substance from which every substance has its being was taken from me. My desire now was not to be more sure of You but more steadfast in You.

But in my temporal life all was uncertain; my heart had to be purged of the old leaven. The way, our Savior himself, delighted me; but I still shrank from actually walking a way so strait. Then by You it came into my mind, and the idea appealed strongly to me, to go to Simplicianus whom I knew to be Your good servant, for Your grace shone in him. I had heard that from his youth he had lived in great love of You. He was now grown old; and it seemed to me that from a long lifetime spent in so firm a following of Your way he must have experienced much and learned much. And truly so it was. I hoped that if I conferred with him about my problems he might from that experience and learning show me the best way for one affected as I was to walk in Your path.

For I saw the Church full; and one went this way, and one that. But I was unhappy at the life I led in the world, and it was indeed a heavy burden, for the hope of honor and profit no longer inflamed my desire, as formerly, to help me bear so exacting a servitude. These things delighted me no longer in comparison with Your sweetness and the beauty of Your house which I loved. But what still held me tight bound was my need of woman: nor indeed did the apostle forbid me to marry, though he exhorted to a better state, wishing all men to be as he was himself. But I in my weakness was for choosing the softer place, and this one thing kept me from taking a sure line upon others. I was weary and wasted with the cares that were eating into me, all because there were many things which I was unwilling to suffer but had to put up with for the sake of living with a wife, a way of life to which I was utterly bound. I had heard from the mouth of Truth itself that *there are eunuchs who have made themselves eunuchs for the kingdom of heaven*; but Christ had said, *He that can take it, let him take it.*

Certainly *all men are vain in whom there is not the knowledge of God and who cannot, by these good things that are seen, find Him that is.* Now I was no longer in that sort of vanity; I had gone beyond it and in the testimony of the whole creation I had found You, our Creator, and Your Word who is with You and one God with You, by whom You created all things. But there is another sort of godlessness, that of the men who *knowing God have not glorified Him as God or given thanks.* Into this also I had fallen, but Your right hand upheld me and taking me out of it, placed me where I might find health. For You have said to man: *Behold, the fear of the Lord is wisdom;* and again: *Be not desirous to seem wise, for those who affirm themselves to be wise become fools.* I had now found the pearl of great price, and I ought to have sold all I had and bought it. But I hesitated still.

II

So I went to Simplicianus, who had begotten Ambrose, now bishop, into Your grace, and whom indeed Ambrose loved as a father. I told him all the wanderings of my error. But when I told him that I had read certain books of the Platonists which had been translated into Latin by Victorinus, one time professor of Rhetoric in Rome—who had, so I heard, died a Christian—he congratulated me for not having fallen upon the writings of other philosophers which are full of vain deceits, according to the elements of this world, whereas in the Platonists God and his Word are everywhere implied. Then to draw me on to the humility of Christ, hidden from the wise and revealed to little ones, he began to speak of Victorinus himself whom he had known intimately when he was in Rome. Of Victorinus he told me what I shall now set down, for the story glorifies Your grace and it should be told to Your glory. For here was an old man deeply learned, trained in all the liberal sciences, a man who had read and weighed so many of the philosophers' writings, the teacher of so many distinguished senators, a man who on account of the brilliance of His teaching had earned and been granted a statue in the Roman forum—an honour the citizens of this world think so great. He had

75 grown old in the worship of idols, had taken part in their sacrilegious rites, for almost all the Roman nobility at that time was enthusiastic for them and was ever talking of "prodigies and the monster gods of every kind, and of the jackal-headed Anubis—who all had once fought against the Roman deities Neptune and Venus and Minerva" and had been beaten: yet Rome was on its knees before these gods it

80 had conquered. All this Victorinus with his thunder of eloquence had gone on championing for so many years even into old age: yet he thought it no shame to be the child of Your Christ, an infant at Your font, bending his neck under the yoke of humility and his forehead to the ignominy of the Cross.

85 O Lord, Lord, who dost *bow down Thy heavens and descend, dost touch the mountains and they smoke,* by what means didst Thou find thy way into that breast? He read, so Simplicianus said, Holy Scripture; he investigated all the Christian writings most carefully and minutely. And he said not publicly but to Simplicianus privately and

90 as one friend to another: "I would have you know that I am now a Christian." Simplicianus answered: "I shall not believe it nor count you among Christians unless I see you in the Church of Christ." Victorinus asked with some faint mockery: "Then is it the walls that make Christians?" He went on saying that he was a Christian, and

95 Simplicianus went on with the same denial, and Victorinus always repeated his retort about the walls. The fact was that he feared to offend his friends, important people and worshippers of these demons; he feared that their enmity might fall heavily upon him from the height of their Babylon-dignity as from the cedars of Lebanon

100 which the Lord had not yet brought down. But when by reading in all earnestness he had drawn strength, he grew afraid that Christ might deny him before His angels if he were ashamed to confess Christ before men. He felt that he was guilty of a great crime in being ashamed of the sacraments of the lowliness of Your Word, when he

105 had not been ashamed of the sacrilegious rites of those demons of pride whom in his pride he had worshipped. So he grew proud towards vanity and humble towards truth. Quite suddenly and with-

out warning he said to Simplicianus, as Simplicianus told me: "Let us go to the Church. I wish to be made a Christian." Simplicianus, unable to control his joy, went with him. He was instructed in the 110 first mysteries of the faith, and not long after gave in his name that he might be regenerated by baptism, to the astonishment of Rome and the joy of the Church. The proud saw it and were enraged, ground their teeth and were livid with envy: but the Lord God was the hope of his servant, so that he had no regard for vanities and lying follies. 115

Finally when the hour had come for his profession of faith—which at Rome was usually made by those who were about to enter into Your grace in a set form of words learned and memorized and spoken from a platform in the sight of the faithful—Simplicianus told me that the priests offered Victorinus to let him make the profession in 120 private, as the custom was with such as seemed likely to find the ordeal embarrassing. But he preferred to make profession of salvation in the sight of the congregation in church. For there had been no salvation in the Rhetoric he had taught, yet he had professed it publicly. Obviously therefore he should be in less fear of Your meek flock when 125 he was uttering Your word, since he had had no fear of the throng of the deluded when uttering his own. When therefore he had gone up to make his profession all those who knew him began whispering his name to one another with congratulatory murmurs. And indeed who there did not know him? And from the lips of the rejoicing congregation sounded the whisper, "Victorinus, Victorinus." They were 130 quick to utter their exultation at seeing him and as quickly fell silent to hear him. He uttered the true faith with glorious confidence, and they would gladly have snatched him to their very heart. Indeed, they did take him to their heart in their love and their joy: with those hands they took him.

III

135

O loving God, what is it in men that makes them rejoice more for the salvation of a soul that was despaired of or one delivered from a major peril, than if there had always been hope or the peril had been less?

140 Even You, O Merciful Father, rejoice more *upon one sinner doing penance than upon ninety and nine just who need not penance.* It is with special joy that we hear how the lost sheep is brought home upon the exultant shoulders of the shepherd and how the coin is put back into Your treasury while the neighbors rejoice with the woman who found it. And the joy we feel at mass in Your church brings tears as we hear

145 of that younger son who was dead and made alive again, who had been lost and was found. You rejoice in us and in Your angels who stand fast in holy charity. For You are ever the same because You ever know, and in the one way of knowing, all those things which are not always existent nor always the same.

150 What is it in the soul, I ask again, that makes it delight more to have found or regained the things it loves than if it had always had them? Creatures other than man bear the same witness, and all things are filled with testimonies acclaiming that it is so. The victorious general has his triumph; but he would not have been victorious if he had

155 not fought; and the greater danger there was in the battle, the greater rejoicing in the triumph. The storm tosses the sailors and threatens to wreck the ship; all are pale with the threat of death. But the sky grows clear, the sea calm, and now they are as wild with exultation as before with fear. A friend is sick and his pulse threatens danger; all who want

160 him well feel as if they shared his sickness. He begins to recover, though he cannot yet walk as strongly as of old: and there is more joy than there was before, when he was still well and could walk properly. Note too that men procure the actual pleasures of human life by way of pain—I mean not only the pain that comes upon us unlooked for

165 and beyond our will, but unpleasantness planned and willingly accepted. There is no pleasure in eating or drinking, unless the discomfort of hunger and thirst come before. Drunkards eat salty things to develop a thirst so great as to be painful, and pleasure arises when the liquor quenches the pain of the thirst. And it is the custom that

170 promised brides do not give themselves at once lest the husband should hold the gift cheap unless delay had set him craving.

We see this in base and dishonorable pleasure, but also in the pleasure that is licit and permitted, and again in the purest and most honourable friendship. We have seen it in the case of him who had been dead and was brought back to life, who had been lost and was found. Universally the greater joy is heralded by greater pain. What does this mean, O Lord my God, when Thou art an eternal joy to Thyself, Thou Thyself art joy itself, and things about Thee ever rejoice in Thee? What does it mean that this part of creation thus alternates between need felt and need met, between discord and harmony? Is this their mode of being, this what Thou didst give them, when from the heights of heaven to the lowest earth, from the beginning of time to the end, from the angel to the worm, from the first movement to the last, Thou didst set all kinds of good things and all Thy just works each in its place, each in its season? Alas for me, how high art Thou in the highest, how deep in the deepest! And Thou dost never depart from us, yet with difficulty do we return to Thee.

IV

Come, Lord, work upon us, call us back, set us on fire and clasp us close, be fragrant to us, draw us to Thy loveliness: let us love, let us run to Thee. Do not many from a deeper pit of blindness than Victorinus come back to Thee, enlightened by that light in which they receive from Thee the power to be made Thy sons? But because they are not so well-known, there is less rejoicing over them even by those who do know them. For when many rejoice together, the joy of each one is richer: they warm themselves at each other's flame. Further in so far as they are known widely, they guide many to salvation and are bound to be followed by many. So that even those who have gone before rejoice much on their account, because the rejoicing is not only on their account. It would be shameful if in Your tabernacle the persons of the rich should be welcome before the poor, or the nobly born before the rest: since Thou has rather chosen the weak things of the world to confound the strong, and hast chosen the base things of the world and the things that are contemptible, and things that are

205 not, in order to bring to nought things that are. It was by Paul's
tongue that You uttered these words. Yet when Paulus the proconsul
came under the light yoke of Christ and became a simple subject of
the great King, his pride brought low by the apostle's spiritual might,
even that least of Your apostles now desired to be called Paul, in place
of his former name of Saul, for the glory of so great a victory. Victory

210 over the enemy is greater when we win from him a man whom he
holds more strongly and through whom he holds more people. He
has a firmer hold on the eminent by reason of their noble rank, and
through them he holds very many people by reason of their authority. Therefore the heart of Victorinus was all the more welcome

215 because the devil had held it as an impregnable fortress; and the
tongue of Victorinus because it was a strong sharp weapon with
which the devil had slain many. It was right for Your sons to rejoice
with more abounding joy because our King had bound the strong
man, and they saw his vessels taken from him and cleansed and made

220 available unto Your honor and *profitable table to the Lord unto every
good work.*

V

Now when this man of Yours, Simplicianus, had told me the story of
Victorinus, I was on fire to imitate him: which indeed was why he
had told me. He added that in the time of the emperor Julian, when

225 a law was made prohibiting Christians from teaching Literature and
Rhetoric, Victorinus had obeyed the law, preferring to give up his
own school of words rather than Your word, by which You make eloquent the tongues of babes. In this he seemed to me not only
courageous but actually fortunate, because it gave him the chance to

230 devote himself wholly to You. I longed for the same chance, but I was
bound not with the iron of another's chains, but by my own iron will.
The enemy held my will; and of it he made a chain and bound me.
Because my will was perverse it changed to lust, and lust yielded to
became habit, and habit not resisted became necessity. These were

235 like links hanging one on another—which is why I have called it a

chain—and their hard bondage held me bound hand and foot. The new will which I now began to have, by which I willed to worship You freely and to enjoy You, O God, the only certain Joy, was not yet strong enough to overcome that earlier will rooted deep through the years. My two wills, one old, one new, one carnal, one spiritual, were 240 in conflict and in their conflict wasted my soul.

Thus, with myself as object of the experiment, I came to understand what I had read, how the *flesh lusts against the spirit and the spirit against the flesh*. I indeed was in both camps, but more in that which I approved in myself than in that which I disapproved. For in 245 a sense it was now no longer I that was in this second camp, because in large part I rather suffered it unwillingly than did it with my will. Yet habit had grown stronger against me by my own act, since I had come willingly where I did not now will to be. Who can justly complain when just punishment overtakes the sinner? I no longer had the 250 excuse which I used to think I had for not yet forsaking the world and serving You, the excuse namely that I had no certain knowledge of the truth. By now I was quite certain; but I was still bound to earth and refused to take service in Your army; I feared to be freed of all the things that impeded me, as strongly as I ought to have feared the 255 being impeded by them. I was held down as agreeably by this world's baggage as one often is by sleep; and indeed the thoughts with which I meditated upon You were like the efforts of a man who wants to get up but is so heavy with sleep that he simply sinks back into it again. There is no one who wants to be asleep always—for every sound 260 judgment holds that it is best to be awake—yet a man often postpones the effort of shaking himself awake when he feels a sluggish heaviness in the limbs, and settles pleasurably into another doze though he knows he should not, because it is time to get up. Similarly I regarded it as settled that it would be better to give myself to Your 265 love rather than go on yielding to my own lust; but the first course delighted and convinced my mind, the second delighted my body and held it in bondage. For there was nothing I could reply when You called me: *Rise, thou that sleepest and arise from the dead: and Christ* 270

shall enlighten thee; and whereas You showed me by every evidence that Your words were true, there was simply nothing I could answer save only laggard lazy words: "Soon," "Quite soon," "Give me just a little while." But "soon" and "quite soon" did not mean any particu-
275 lar time; and "just a little while" went on for a long while. It was in vain that *I delighted in Thy law according to the inner man, when that other law in my members rebelled against the law of my mind and led me captive in the law of sin that was in my members.* For the law of sin is the fierce force of habit, by which the mind is drawn and held even
280 against its will, and yet deservedly because it had fallen wilfully into the habit. *Who then should deliver me from the body of this death, but Thy grace only, through Jesus Christ Our Lord?*

VI

Now, O Lord, my Helper and my Redeemer, I shall tell and confess to Your name how You delivered me from the chain of that desire of
285 the flesh which held me so bound, and the servitude of worldly things. I went my usual way with a mind ever more anxious, and day after day I sighed for You. I would be off to Your church as often as my business, under the weight of which I groaned, left me free. Alypius was with me, at liberty from his legal office after a third term as
290 Assessor and waiting for private clients, to whom he might sell his legal advice—just as I sold skill in speaking, if indeed this can be bought. Nebridius had yielded to our friendship so far as to teach under Verecundus, a great friend of all of us, a citizen and elementary school teacher of Milan, who had earnestly asked and indeed by right
295 of friendship demanded from our company the help he badly needed. Nebridius was not influenced in the matter by any desire for profit, for he could have done better had he chosen, in a more advanced school; but he was a good and gracious friend and too kindly a man to refuse our requests. But he did it all very quietly, for he did not
300 want to draw the attention of those persons whom the world holds great; he thus avoided distraction of mind, for he wanted to have his mind free and at leisure for as many hours as possible to seek or read or hear truths concerning wisdom.

On a certain day—Nebridius was away for some reason I cannot recall—there came to Alypius and me at our house one Ponticianus, 305 a fellow countryman of ours, being from Africa, holder of an important post in the emperor's court. There was something or other he wanted of us and we sat down to discuss the matter. As it happened he noticed a book on a gaming table by which we were sitting. He picked it up, opened it, and found that it was the apostle Paul, which 310 surprised him because he had expected that it would be one of the books I wore myself out teaching. Then he smiled a little and looked at me, and expressed pleasure but surprise too at having come suddenly upon that book, and only that book, lying before me. For he was a Christian and a devout Christian; he knelt before You in 315 church, O our God, in daily prayer and many times daily. I told him that I had given much care to these writings. Whereupon he began to tell the story of the Egyptian monk Antony, whose name was held in high honor among Your servants, although Alypius and I had never heard it before that time. When he learned this, he was the more 320 intent upon telling the story, anxious to introduce so great a man to men ignorant of him, and very much marvelling at our ignorance. But Alypius and I stood amazed to hear of Your wonderful works, done in the true faith and in the Catholic Church so recently, practically in our own times, and with such numbers of witnesses. All three 325 of us were filled with wonder, we because the deeds we were now hearing were so great, and he because we had never heard them before.

From this story he went on to the great groups in the monasteries, and their ways all redolent of You, and the fertile deserts of the wilderness, of all of which we knew nothing. There was actually a monastery 330 at Milan, outside the city walls. It was full of worthy brethren and under the care of Ambrose. And we had not heard of it. He continued with his discourse and we listened in absolute silence. It chanced that he told how on one occasion he and three of his companions— 335 it was at Treves, when the emperor was at the chariot races in the Circus—had gone one afternoon to walk in the gardens close by the city walls. As it happened they fell into two groups, one of the others staying with him, and the other two likewise walking their own way. 340 But as those other two strolled on they came into a certain house, the dwelling of some servants of Yours, poor in spirit, of whom is the kingdom of God. There they found a small book in which was written the life of Antony. One of them began to read it, marvelled at it, was inflamed by it. While he was actually reading he had begun to 345 think how he might embrace such a life, and give up his worldly employment to serve You alone. For the two men were both state officials. Suddenly the man who was doing the reading was filled with a love of holiness and angry at himself with righteous shame. He looked at his friend and said to him: "Tell me, please, what is the goal 350 of our ambition in all these labors of ours? What are we aiming at? What is our motive in being in the public service? Have we any higher hope at court than to be friends of the emperor? And at that level, is not everything uncertain and full of perils? And how many perils must we meet on the way to this greater peril? And how long 355 before we are there? But if I should choose to be a friend of God, I can become one now." He said this, and all troubled with the pain of the new life coming to birth in him, he turned back his eyes to the book. He read on and was changed inwardly, where You alone could see; and the world dropped away from his mind, as soon appeared 360 outwardly. For while he was reading and his heart thus tossing on its own flood, at length he broke out in heavy weeping, saw the better way and chose it for his own. Being now Your servant he said to his friend, "Now I have broken from that hope we had and have decided to serve God; and I enter upon that service from this hour, in this 365 place. If you have no will to imitate me, at least do not try to dissuade me."

The other replied that he would remain his companion in so great a service for so great a prize. So the two of them, now Your servants, built a spiritual tower at the only cost that is adequate, the cost of 370 leaving all things and following You. Then Ponticianus and the man who had gone walking with him in another part of the garden came

looking for them in the same place, and when they found them suggested that they should return home as the day was now declining.
But they told their decision and their purpose, and how that will had
arisen in them; and was now settled in them; and asked them not to
try to argue them out of their decision, even if they would not also
join them. Ponticianus and his friend, though not changed from their
former state, yet wept for themselves, as he told us, and congratulated
them in God and commended themselves to their prayers. Then with
their own heart trailing in the dust they went off to the palace, while
the other two, with their heart fixed upon heaven, remained in the
hut. Both these men, as it happened, were betrothed, and when the
two women heard of it they likewise dedicated their virginity to You.

VII

This was the story Ponticianus told. But You, Lord, while he was
speaking, turned me back towards myself, taking me from behind my
own back where I had put myself all the time that I preferred not to
see myself. And You set me there before my own face that I might see
how vile I was, how twisted and unclean and spotted and ulcerous. I
saw myself and was horrified; but there was no way to flee from
myself. If I tried to turn my gaze from myself, there was Ponticianus
telling what he was telling; and again You were setting me face to face
with myself, forcing me upon my own sight, that I might see my
iniquity and loathe it. I had known it, but I had pretended not to see
it, had deliberately looked the other way and let it go from my mind.
But this time, the more ardently I approved those two as I heard of
their determination to win health for their souls by giving themselves
up wholly to Your healing, the more detestable did I find myself in
comparison with them. For many years had flowed by—a dozen or
more—from the time when I was nineteen and was stirred by the
reading of Cicero's Hortensius to the study of wisdom; and here was
I still postponing the giving up of this world's happiness to devote
myself to the search for that of which not the finding only but the
mere seeking is better than to find all the treasures and kingdoms of

375

380

385

390

395

400

405 men, better than all the body's pleasures though they were to be had merely for a nod. But I in my great worthlessness—for it was greater thus early—had begged You for chastity, saying: "Grant me chastity and continence, but not yet." For I was afraid that You would hear my prayer too soon, and too soon would heal me from the disease of lust which I wanted satisfied rather than extinguished. So I had gone

410 wandering in my sacrilegious superstition through the base ways of the Manicheans: not indeed that I was sure they were right but that I preferred them to the Christians, whom I did not inquire about in the spirit of religion but simply opposed through malice.

I had thought that my reason for putting off from day to day the

415 following of You alone to the contempt of earthly hopes was that I did not see any certain goal towards which to direct my course. But now the day was come when I stood naked in my own sight and my conscience accused me: "Why is my voice not heard? Surely you are the man who used to say that you could not cast off vanity's baggage for

420 an uncertain truth. Very well: now the truth is certain, yet you are still carrying the load. Here are men who have been given wings to free their shoulders from the load, though they did not wear themselves out in searching nor spend ten years or more thinking about it."

Thus was I inwardly gnawed at. And I was in the grip of the most

425 horrible and confounding shame, while Ponticianus was telling his story. He finished the tale and the business for which he had come; and he went his way, and I to myself. What did I not say against myself, with what lashes of condemnation did I not scourge my soul to make it follow me now that I wanted to follow You! My soul hung

430 back. It would not follow, yet found no excuse for not following. All its arguments had already been used and refuted. There remained only trembling silence: for it feared as very death the cessation of that habit of which in truth it was dying.

VIII

In the midst of that great tumult of my inner dwelling place, the

435 tumult I had stirred up against my own soul in the chamber of my

heart, I turned upon Alypius, wild in look and troubled in mind, crying out: "What is wrong with us? What is this that you heard? The unlearned arise and take heaven by force, and here are we with all our learning, stuck fast in flesh and blood! Is there any shame in following because they have gone before us, would it not be a worse shame not to follow at once?" These words and more of the same sort I uttered, then the violence of my feeling tore me from him while he stood staring at me thunderstruck. For I did not sound like myself. My brow, cheeks, eyes, flush, the pitch of my voice, spoke my mind more powerfully than the words I uttered. There was a garden attached to our lodging, of which we had the use, as indeed we had of the whole house: for our host, the master of the house, did not live there. To this garden the storm in my breast somehow brought me, for there no one could intervene in the fierce suit I had brought against myself, until it should reach its issue: though what the issue was to be, You knew, not I: but there I was, going mad on my way to sanity, dying on my way to life, aware how evil I was, unaware that I was to grow better in a little while. So I went off to the garden, and Alypius close on my heels: for it was still privacy for me to have him near, and how could he leave me to myself in that state? We found a seat as far as possible from the house. I was frantic in mind, in a frenzy of indignation at myself for not going over to Your law and Your covenant, O my God, where all my bones cried out that I should be, extolling it to the skies. The way was not by ship or chariot or on foot: it was not as far as I had gone when I went from the house to the place where we sat. For I had but to will to go, in order not merely to go but to arrive: I had only to will to go—but to will powerfully and wholly, not to turn and twist a will half-wounded this way and that, with the part that would rise struggling against the part that would keep to the earth.

In the torment of my irresolution, I did many bodily acts. Now men sometimes will to do bodily acts but cannot, whether because they have not the limbs, or because their limbs are bound or weakened with illness or in some other way unable to act. If I tore my hair,

470 if I beat my forehead, if I locked my fingers and clasped my knees, I
did it because I willed to. But I might have willed and yet not done
it, if my limbs had not had the pliability to do what I willed. Thus I
did so many things where the will to do them was not at all the same
thing as the power to do them: and I did not do what would have

475 pleased me incomparably more to do—a thing too which I could
have done as soon as I willed to, given that willing means willing
wholly. For in that matter, the power was the same thing as the will,
and the willing *was* the doing. Yet it was not done, and the body more
readily obeyed the slightest wish of the mind, more readily moved its

480 limbs at the mind's mere nod, than the mind obeyed itself in carrying out its own great will which could be achieved simply by willing.

IX

Why this monstrousness? And what is the root of it? Let Your mercy
enlighten me, that I may put the question: whether perhaps the
answer lies in the mysterious punishment that has come upon men

485 and some deeply hidden damage in the sons of Adam. Why this monstrousness? And what is the root of it? The mind gives the body an
order, and is obeyed at once: the mind gives itself an order and is
resisted. The mind commands the hand to move and there is such
readiness that you can hardly distinguish the command from its exe-

490 cution. Yet the mind is mind, whereas the hand is body. The mind
commands the mind to will, the mind is itself, but it does not do it.
Why this monstrousness? And what is the root of it? The mind I say
commands itself to will: it would not give the command unless it
willed: yet it does not do what it commands. The trouble is that it

495 does not totally will: therefore it does not totally command. It commands in so far as it wills; and it disobeys the command in so far as
it does not will. The will is commanding itself to be a will—commanding itself, not some other. But it does not in its fullness give the
command, so that what it commands is not done. For if the will were

500 so in its fullness, it would not command itself to will, for it would
already will. It is therefore no monstrousness, partly to will, partly not

to will, but a sickness of the soul to be so weighted down by custom that it cannot wholly rise even with the support of truth. Thus there are two wills in us, because neither of them is entire: and what is lacking to the one is present in the other.

X

505

Let them perish from thy presence, O God, as perish vain talkers and seducers of the soul, who observing that there are two wills at issue in our coming to a decision proceed to assert [as the Manichees do] that there are two minds in us of different natures, one good, one evil. For they are evil themselves in holding such evil opinions; and they will 510 become good only if they perceive truth and come to it as your Apostle says to them: *You were heretofore darkness but now light in the Lord.* But these men though they want to be light, want to be light in themselves and not in the Lord, imagining the nature of the soul to be the same as God. Thus they become not light but deeper darkness, since 515 in their abominable arrogance they have gone further from You, *the true Light that enlightens every man that comes into this world.* Take heed what you say and blush for shame: *draw near unto Him and be enlightened, and your faces shall not be ashamed.* When I was deliberating about serving the Lord my God, as I had long meant to do, it 520 was I who willed to do it, I who was unwilling. It was I. I did not wholly will, I was not wholly unwilling. Therefore I strove with myself and was distracted by myself. This distraction happened to me though I did not want it, and it showed me not the presence of some second mind, but the punishment of my own mind. Thus it was not 525 I who caused it but *the sin that dwells in me,* the punishment of a sin freely committed by Adam, whose son I am.

For if there be as many contrary natures in man as there are wills in conflict with one another, then there are not two natures in us but several. Take the case of a man trying to make up his mind whether 530 he would go to the Manichees' meeting-house or to the theater. The Manichees would say: "Here you have two natures, one good, bringing him to the meeting-house, the other evil, taking him away. How

535 else could you have this wavering between two wills pulling against each other?" Now I say that both are bad, the will that would take him to the Manichees and the will that would take him to the theater. But they hold that the will by which one comes to them is good. Very well! Supposing one of us is trying to decide and wavering between two wills in conflict, whether to go to the theater or to our

540 church, will not the Manichees be in some trouble about an answer? For either they must admit, which they do not want to, that a good will would take a man to our church as they think it is a good will that brings those who are receivers of their sacrament and belong to them to their church; or they must hold that there are two evil natures

545 and two evil wills at conflict in one man, and what they are always saying will not be true—namely that there is one good will and one evil will. Otherwise, they must be converted to the truth and not deny that when a man is taking a decision there is one soul drawn this way and that by diverse wills.

550 Therefore, when they perceive that there are two wills in conflict in man, they must not say that there are two opposing minds in conflict, one good, one bad, from two opposing substances and two opposing principles. For you, O God of truth, refute them and disprove them and convict them of error: as in the case where both wills

555 are bad, when, for instance, a man is deliberating whether he shall kill another man by poison or by dagger; whether he should seize this or that part of another man's property, when he cannot seize both; whether he should spend his money on lust or hoard his money through avarice; whether he should go to the games or the theater if

560 they happen both to come on the same day. Let us add a third possibility to this last man, whether he should go and commit a theft from someone else's house, if the occasion should arise: and indeed a fourth, whether he should go and commit adultery, if the chance occurs at the same time. If all four things come together at the same

570 point of time, and all are equally desired, yet all cannot be done, then they tear the mind by the conflicting pull of four wills—or even more, given the great mass of things which can be desired. Yet the Manichees do not hold such a multitude of different substances.

The same reasoning applies to wills that are good. For I ask them whether it is good to find delight in the reading of the Apostle, and good to find delight in the serenity of a Psalm, and good to discuss the Gospel. To each of these they answer that it is good: but, if all these things attract us at the same moment, are not different wills tugging at the heart of man while we deliberate which we should choose? Thus they are all good, yet they are all in conflict until one is chosen, and then the whole will is at rest and at one, whereas it had been divided into many. Or again, when eternity attracts the higher faculties and the pleasure of some temporal good holds the lower, it is one same soul that wills both, but not either with its whole will; and it is therefore torn both ways and deeply troubled while truth shows the one way as better but habit keeps it to the other.

XI

Thus I was sick at heart and in torment, accusing myself with a new intensity of bitterness, twisting and turning in my chain in the hope that it might be utterly broken, for what held me was so small a thing! But it still held me. And You stood in the secret places of my soul, O Lord, in the harshness of Your mercy redoubling the scourges of fear and shame lest I should give way again and that small slight tie which remained should not be broken but should grow again to full strength and bind me closer even than before. For I kept saying within myself: "Let it be now, let it be now," and by the mere words I had begun to move towards the resolution. I almost made it, yet I did not quite make it. But I did not fall back into my original state, but as it were stood near to get my breath. And I tried again and I was almost there, and now I could all but touch it and hold it: yet I was not quite there, I did not touch it or hold it. I still shrank from dying unto death and living unto life. The lower condition which had grown habitual was more powerful than the better condition which I had not tried. The nearer the point of time came in which I was to become different, the more it struck me with horror; but it did not force me utterly back nor turn me utterly away, but held me there between the two.

575

580

585

590

595

600

605

Those trifles of all trifles, and vanities of vanities, my one-time mistresses, held me back, plucking at my garment of flesh and murmuring softly: "Are you sending us away?" And "From this moment shall we not be with you, now or forever?" And "From this moment
610 shall this or that not be allowed you, now or forever?" What were they suggesting to me in the phrase I have written "this or that," what were they suggesting to me, O my God? Do you in your mercy keep from the soul of Your servant the vileness and uncleanness they were suggesting. And now I began to hear them not half so loud; they no
615 longer stood against me face to face, but were softly muttering behind my back and, as I tried to depart, plucking stealthily at me to make me look behind. Yet even that was enough, so hesitating was I, to keep me from snatching myself free, from shaking them off and leaping upwards on the way I was called: for the strong force of habit said
620 to me: "Do you think you can live without them?"

But by this time its voice was growing fainter. In the direction towards which I had turned my face and was quivering in fear of going, I could see the austere beauty of Continence, serene and indeed joyous but not evilly, honorably soliciting me to come to her
625 and not linger, stretching forth loving hands to receive and embrace me, hands full of multitudes of good examples. With her I saw such hosts of young men and maidens, a multitude of youth and of every age, gray widows and women grown old in virginity, and in them all Continence herself, not barren but the fruitful mother of children,
630 her joys, by You, Lord, her Spouse. And she smiled upon me and her smile gave courage as if she were saying: "Can you not do what these men have done, what these women have done? Or could men or women have done such in themselves, and not in the Lord their God? The Lord their God gave me to them. Why do you stand upon your-
635 self and so not stand at all? Cast yourself upon Him and be not afraid; He will not draw away and let you fall. Cast yourself without fear, He will receive you and heal you."

Yet I was still ashamed, for I could still hear the murmuring of those vanities, and I still hung hesitant. And again it was as if she said:

"Stop your ears against your unclean members, that they may be mor-   640
tified. They tell you of delights, but not of such delights as the law of
the Lord your God tells." This was the controversy raging in my
heart, a controversy about myself against myself. And Alypius stayed
by my side and awaited in silence the issue of such agitation as he had
never seen in me.

XII
                                                                            645

When my most searching scrutiny had drawn up all my vileness from
the secret depths of my soul and heaped it in my heart's sight, a
mighty storm arose in me, bringing a mighty rain of tears. That I
might give way to my tears and lamentations, I rose from Alypius: for
it struck me that solitude was more suited to the business of weeping.   650
I went far enough from him to prevent his presence from being an
embarrassment to me. So I felt, and he realized it. I suppose I had said
something and the sound of my voice was heavy with tears. I arose,
but he remained where we had been sitting, still in utter amazement.
I flung myself down somehow under a certain fig tree and no longer   655
tried to check my tears, which poured forth from my eyes in a flood,
an acceptable sacrifice to Thee. And much I said not in these words but
to this effect: *"And Thou, O, Lord, how long? How long, Lord; wilt
Thou be angry forever? Remember not our former iniquities."* For I felt
that I was still bound by them. And I continued my miserable com-   660
plaining: "How long, how long shall I go on saying tomorrow and
again tomorrow? Why not now, why not have an end to my uncleanness this very hour?"

Such things I said, weeping in the most bitter sorrow of my heart.
And suddenly I heard a voice from some nearby house, a boy's voice   665
or a girl's voice, I do not know: but it was a sort of sing-song, repeated
again and again, "Take and read, take and read." I ceased weeping and
immediately began to search my mind most carefully as to whether
children were accustomed to chant these words in any kind of game,
and I could not remember that I had ever heard any such thing.   670
Damming back the flood of my tears I arose, interpreting the incident

as quite certainly a divine command to open my book of Scripture and read the passage at which I should open. For it was part of what I had been told about Anthony, that from the Gospel which he hap-
675 pened to be reading he had felt that he was being admonished as though what he read was spoken directly to himself: *Go, sell what thou hast and give to the poor and thou shalt have treasure in heaven; and come follow Me.* By this experience he had been in that instant converted to You. So I was moved to return to the place where Alyp-
680 ius was sitting, for I had put down the Apostle's book there when I arose. I snatched it up, opened it and in silence read the passage upon which my eyes first fell: *Not in rioting and drunkenness, not in chambering and impurities, not in contention and envy, but put ye on the Lord Jesus Christ and make not provision for the flesh in its concupis-*
685 *cences. [Romans xiii, 13.]* I had no wish to read further, and no need. For in that instant, with the very ending of the sentence, it was as though a light of utter confidence shone in all my heart, and all the darkness of uncertainty vanished away. Then leaving my finger in the place or marking it by some other sign, I closed the book and in com-
690 plete calm told the whole thing to Alypius and he similarly told me what had been going on in himself, of which I knew nothing. He asked to see what I had read. I showed him, and he looked further than I had read. I had not known what followed. And this is what followed: *"Now him that is weak in faith, take unto you."* He applied this
695 to himself and told me so. And he was confirmed by this message, and with no troubled wavering gave himself to God's good-will and purpose—a purpose indeed most suited to his character, for in these matters he had been immeasurably better than I.

Then we went in to my mother and told her, to her great joy. We
700 related how it had come about: she was filled with triumphant exultation, and praised You who are mighty beyond what we ask or conceive: for she saw that You had given her more than with all her pitiful weeping she had ever asked. For You converted me to Yourself so that I no longer sought a wife nor any of this world's promises, but
705 stood upon that same rule of faith in which You had shown me to her

so many years before. Thus You changed her mourning into joy, a joy far richer than she had thought to wish, a joy much dearer and purer than she had thought to find in grandchildren of my flesh.

12

Against Inconoclasm
(An Excerpt)

COUNCIL OF NICAEA 11 (A.D. 787)

INTRODUCTION

A controversy raged in Eastern Christianity from ca. A.D. 725 to 842
on whether it is permitted according to the Christian faith to venerate sacred images or "icons" (Gk: *eikôn*) of God and the saints. The
Monophysite heresy that minimized the humanity of Jesus, the
Manichaean Paulicians who tended to see all matter as evil, and possibly also Islam which condemned all attempts to create images of the
divine, probably contributed to a movement to remove and destroy
all sacred images in Christian churches. Emperor Leo III the Isaurian
(717–741) regarded icons as the chief obstacle to the conversion of
Jews and Muslims, and so to bringing peace and unity to his realm.
In 726 he therefore declared all icons "idols" and ordered them
destroyed. St. Germanus, Patriarch of Constantinople, opposed the
decree and so was deposed. And monks, the most ardent iconodules,

were severely persecuted. Leo's son, Constantine V, succeeded him in 741 and continued the iconoclast policy. However, Constantine's son Leo IV (775–80) was less adamant. After his death his wife, the Empress Irene, regent for her young son Constantine, reversed the policy and in 787 called the Council of Nicaea II.

That council issued a decree—a selection from which is included here—in which it defined the degree of veneration due to icons and demanded their restoration throughout the empire. Nevertheless, the army remained opposed to icons, causing a second period of iconoclasm that began in 814 and resulted in much destruction and bloodshed. This persecution ended only after the death of Emperor Theophilus in 842. When his widow, Theodora, regent for her young son, had Methodius elected Patriarch in 843, a great feast was inaugurated on the first Sunday of Lent in honor of icons, known ever since as the "Feast of Orthodoxy."

Well before the controversy, Leontius of Neapolis (Cyprus, ca. 590–650) wrote a work on sacred images in which he sets forth a theology of humanity's relationship to the created world: "Through heaven and earth and sea, through wood and stone, through relics and church buildings and the Cross, through angels and humans, through all creation visible and invisible, I offer veneration and honor to the Creator and the Master and Maker of all things, and to Him alone. For creation does not venerate the Maker directly and by itself, but it is through me that the heavens declare the glory of God, through me the moon worships God, through me the waters and showers of rain, the dew and all creation, venerate God and give him glory." During the iconoclast period, Doctor of the Church St. John Damascene (ca. 675–749) and St. Theodore of Studios (759–826) both wrote stirringly in defense of icons, also tying them into the Christian doctrines of creation and incarnation. According to Damascene, "The Word made flesh has deified the flesh," so there can be no unbridgeable gap between God and humanity, spiritual and material. Theodore adds, "If merely mental contemplation [of God] were sufficient, it would have been sufficient for him to come to us in a merely mental way."

—Rev. John D. Laurance, S.J.

TEXT

The holy, great, and Ecumenical Synod which by the grace of God and the will of the pious and Christ-loving Emperors, Constantine and Irene, his mother, was gathered together for the second time at Nicaea, the illustrious metropolis of Bithynia, in the holy church of God which is named Sophia, having followed the tradition of the   5
Catholic Church, has defined as follows:

Christ our Lord, who has bestowed upon us the light of the knowledge of himself, and has redeemed us from the darkness of idolatrous madness, having espoused the Holy Catholic Church to himself without spot or defect, promised that he would so preserve her: and gave   10
his word to this effect to his holy disciples when he said: "Behold! I am with you always, even to the end of the world," which promise he made, not only to them, but to us also who should believe in his name through their word. But some, not appreciating this gift, and having become fickle through the temptation of the wily enemy, have   15
fallen from the right faith. For, withdrawing from the traditions of the Catholic Church, they have wandered from the truth and as the proverb says: "The husbandmen have gone astray in their own husbandry and have gathered in their hands nothingness." Certain priests, priests in name only, not in fact, had dared to speak against   20
the God-approved ornament of the sacred monuments, of whom God cries aloud through the prophet, "Many pastors have corrupted my vineyard, they have polluted my portion."

And, indeed, following profane men, led astray by their carnal sense, they have calumniated the Church of Christ, our God, which   25
he has espoused to himself, and have failed to distinguish between holy and profane, referring to the images of our Lord and of his Saints by the same name as the statues of diabolical idols. Seeing all this, our

30 Lord God (not willing to see his people corrupted by this kind of plague) by his good pleasure has called us together, the chief of his priests, from every quarter, moved with a divine zeal and brought here by the will of our princes, Constantine and Irene, so that the traditions of the Catholic Church might be stabilized by our common decree. Therefore, with all diligence, making a thorough examination

35 and analysis, and following the direction of the truth, we subtract nothing, we add nothing, but we preserve unchanged everything that pertains to the Catholic Church, and following the Six Ecumenical Synods, especially that which met in this illustrious metropolis of Nicaea, as well as that which was afterwards gathered together in the

40 God-protected Royal City (Constantinople).

We believe . . . . . . life of the world to come. Amen (*The full Nicene-Constantinopolitan Creed is read*).

* * *

To make our confession short, we keep unchanged all the ecclesiastical traditions handed down to us, whether in writing or verbally, one

45 of which is the making of pictorial representations, agreeable to the history of the preaching of the gospel, a tradition useful in many respects, but especially in this, that so the incarnation of the Word of God is shown forth as real and not merely phantastic, for these have mutual indications and without doubt have also mutual significations.

50 We, therefore, following the royal pathway and the divinely inspired authority of our Holy Fathers and the traditions of the Catholic Church (for, as we all know, the Holy Spirit indwells her), define with all certitude and accuracy that just as the figure of the precious and life-giving Cross, so also the venerable and holy images, as

55 well in painting and mosaic as of other fit materials, should be set forth in the holy churches of God, and on the sacred vessels and on the vestments and on hangings and in pictures both in houses and by the wayside, that is, the figure of our Lord God and Savior Jesus Christ, of our spotless Lady, the Mother of God, of the honorable

60 Angels, of all Saints and of all pious people. For by so much more

Mosaic Showing Christ Pantocrator, from the altar in the Monreale Cathedral, Sicily.
© Scala/Firenze

often as they are seen in artistic representation, by so much more readily are people lifted up to the memory of their prototypes, and to a longing after them; and to these should be given due salutation and honorable reverence, not indeed that true worship of faith (*latreia*)
65 which pertains alone to the divine nature; but to these, as to the figure of the precious and life-giving Cross and to the Book of the Gospels and to the other holy objects, incense and lights may be offered according to ancient pious custom. For the honor which is paid to the image passes on to that which the image represents, and
70 he who reveres the image reveres in it the subject represented. For thus the teaching of our holy Fathers, that is the tradition of the Catholic Church, which from one end of the earth to the other has received the gospel, is strengthened. Thus we follow Paul, who spoke in Christ, and the whole divine Apostolic company and the holy
75 Fathers, holding fast to the traditions which we have received. So we sing prophetically the triumphal hymns of the Church, "Rejoice greatly, O daughter of Sion; Shout, O daughter of Jerusalem. Rejoice and be glad with all your heart. The Lord has taken away from you the oppression of your adversaries; you are redeemed from the hand
80 of your enemies. The Lord is a King in your midst; you will not see evil any more, and peace be to you forever."

Those, therefore who dare to think or teach otherwise, or as wicked heretics to spurn the traditions of the Church and to invent some novelty, or else to reject some of those things which the Church
85 has received (e.g., the Book of the Gospels, or the image of the cross, or the pictorial icons, or the holy relics of a martyr), or evilly and sharply to devise anything subversive of the lawful traditions of the Catholic Church or to turn to common uses the sacred vessels or the venerable monasteries, if they be bishops or clerics, we command
90 that they be deposed; if religious or laity, that they be cut off from communion.

[*After all had signed, the acclamations began.*]

The holy Synod cried out: So we all believe, we all are so minded, we all give our consent and have signed. This is the faith of the Apos-

tles, this is the faith of the Orthodox, this is the faith which has made   95
firm the whole world. Believing in one God, to be celebrated in Trinity, we salute the honorable images! Those who do not so hold, let
them be anathema. Those who do not thus think, let them be driven
far away from the Church. For we follow the most ancient legislation
of the Catholic Church. We keep the laws of the Fathers. We anath-   100
ematize those who add anything to or take anything away from the
Catholic Church. We anathematize the introduced novelty of the
revilers of Christians. We salute the venerable images. We place under
anathema those who do not do this. Anathema to them who presume
to apply to the venerable images the things said in Holy Scripture   105
about idols. Anathema to those who do not salute the holy and venerable images. Anathema to those who call the sacred images idols.
Anathema to those who say that Christians resort to the sacred images
as to gods. Anathema to those who say that any other delivered us
from idols except Christ our God. Anathema to those who dare to say   110
that at any time the Catholic Church received idols.

13

Summa theologiae, I Q.1, art.1: Is Theology Necessary?

THOMAS AQUINAS (1225–1274)

INTRODUCTION

1. Who is Thomas Aquinas and why does his opinion matter to us?

Thomas Aquinas (1224–1274) was a Dominican friar and university professor, who taught courses in Scripture at the recently founded universities of Paris, Rome, and Naples. He is known as a philosopher for his commentaries on the works of Aristotle, and distinguished himself as a theologian with two major summaries of Christian thought, the *Summa contra Gentiles*, and the *Summa theologiae*. Less than fifty years after his death, he was formally recognized as a saint of the Catholic Church. His students called him the "Doctor Angelicus," for his theology of angels; others referred to him as the "Doctor Communis," or common teacher of all Christians.

2. What is the *Summa theologiae?*

The *Summa theologiae* is a multi-volume handbook for beginning students of theology. It is composed of a series of *questions*, or discussion topics, further divided into *articles*, or mini-debates resolving questions raised by Christian doctrine. The first part of the *Summa* deals with the basis of theology, God, the Trinity, providence and predestination, and the creation of the world, angels, and human beings. The next two sections of the *Summa* are called the first part of the second part, and the second part of the second part. The first part of the second part discusses the goals of human existence in terms of human emotion, character development, virtues, and vices, then concludes with a series of questions on sin, the law, and divine grace. The second part of the second part covers the seven virtues and the vices opposed to them. Finally, the third part covers the life of Christ, and the sacraments of his Church.

3. Why is theology necessary?

When you signed up for this course, you may have asked yourself, "why do I have to take theology, when we already discussed the existence of God in our philosophy course?" Doesn't philosophy give us enough information about God? In article one of question one of the *Summa theologiae*, Thomas Aquinas addresses these questions, since his students probably asked them, too.

Thomas Aquinas lets the opponents of theological studies speak first, in two opening arguments; one is from Ecclesiasticus in the Old Testament, the other from Aristotle. He then counters these arguments with a New Testament text, where Scripture is said to be *divinely inspired*, and useful for instruction. Responding to both sides of the argument, he points out that God is beyond the reach of human reason or investigation; to be known to us, God must reveal himself to us. Theology is the study of this divine revelation, which is found in Scripture. Responding to the two opening arguments, Aquinas reiterates that what is inaccessible to reason, can be known through revelation. Different sciences use different methods to study the same objects and arrive at the same conclusions. Hence, there need be no conflict between theology and philosophy when both investigate the existence of God, although theology relies on revelation, and philosophy uses human reason.

The full text of the *Summa theologiae* is available on the internet:

http://www.ccel.org/a/aquinas/summa/

—*Dr. Wanda Zemler-Cizewski*

TEXT

Summa Theologiae, I, 1:
The Nature and Extent of Sacred Doctrine
(In Ten Articles)

To place our purpose within proper limits, we first endeavor to investigate the nature and extent of this sacred doctrine. Concerning this there are ten points of inquiry:—

(1) Whether it is necessary? (2) Whether it is a science? (3) Whether it is one or many? (4) Whether it is speculative or practical? (5) How it is compared with other sciences? (6) Whether it is the same as wisdom? (7) Whether God is its subject-matter? (8) Whether it is a matter of argument? (9) Whether it rightly employs metaphors and similes? (10) Whether the Sacred Scripture of this doctrine may be expounded in different senses?

First Article:

Whether, besides Philosophy,
Any Further Doctrine Is Required?

We proceed thus to the First Article:—

Objection 1. It seems that, besides philosophical science, we have no need of any further knowledge. For man should not seek to know what is above reason: *Seek not the things that are too high for thee* (Eccles. iii. 22). But whatever is not above reason is fully treated of in philosophical science. Therefore any other knowledge besides philosophical science is superfluous.

Chartres Cathedral, France.
Photo by John D. Laurance, S.J.

Obj. 2. Further, knowledge can be concerned only with being, for nothing can be known, save what is true; and all that is, is true. But everything that is, is treated of in philosophical science—even God Himself; so that there is a part of philosophy called theology, or the divine science, as Aristotle has proved (*Metaph.* vi). Therefore, besides philosophical science, there is no need of any further knowledge.

On the contrary, It is written (2 Tim. iii. 16): *All Scripture inspired of God is profitable to teach, to reprove, to correct, to instruct in justice.* Now Scripture, inspired of God, is no part of philosophical science, which has been built up by human reason. Therefore it is useful that besides philosophical science there should be other knowledge—*i.e.,* inspired of God.

I answer that, It was necessary for man's salvation that there should be a knowledge revealed by God, besides philosophical science built up by human reason. Firstly, indeed, because man is directed to God, as to an end that surpasses the grasp of his reason: *The eye hath not seen, O God, besides Thee, what things Thou hast prepared for them that wait for Thee* (Isa. lxvi. 4). But the end must first be known by men who are to direct their thoughts and actions to the end. Hence it was necessary for the salvation of man that certain truths which exceed human reason should be made known to him by divine revelation. Even as regards those truths about God which human reason could have discovered, it was necessary that man should be taught by a divine revelation; because the truth about God such as reason could discover, would only be known by a few, and that after a long time, and with the admixture of many errors. Whereas man's whole salvation, which is in God, depends upon the knowledge of this truth. Therefore, in order that the salvation of men might be brought about more fitly and more surely, it was necessary that they should be taught divine truths by divine revelation. It was therefore necessary that, besides philosophical science built up by reason there should be a sacred science learned through revelation.

50   *Reply Obj. 1.* Although those things which are beyond man's knowledge may not be sought for by man through his reason, nevertheless, once they are revealed by God they must be accepted by faith. Hence the sacred text continues, *For many things are shown to thee above the understanding of man* (Eccles. iii. 25). And in this the sacred

55   science consists.

        Reply Obj. 2. Sciences are differentiated according to the various means through which knowledge is obtained. For the astronomer and the physicist both may prove the same conclusion—that the earth, for instance, is round: the astronomer by means of mathematics (*i.e.,*

60   abstracting from matter), but the physicist by means of matter itself. Hence there is no reason why those things which may be learned from philosophical science, so far as they can be known by natural reason, may not also be taught us by another science so far as they fall within revelation. Hence theology included in sacred doctrine differs

65   in kind from that theology which is part of philosophy.

14

Revelations of Divine Love, 58–60

JULIAN OF NORWICH (1342–ca. 1420)

INTRODUCTION

Julian and Her Writings

The anonymous anchoress who authored the first work by a woman in English is called "Julian" or "Dame Julian," probably after the church to which her monastic cell was attached, in the city of Norwich, England. Julian lived during an era of church turmoil, the plague, the writings of Chaucer, and a flourishing of mysticism. She spent years in prayer and solitude, and was revered as a holy recluse and wise spiritual counselor.

Julian's writings in mystical theology matured over two decades of prayerful contemplation, following sixteen visions or "showings" she experienced in May, 1373, while near death from illness. The visions focus on the Triune God affirmed in the Nicene Creed, and the Christian mysteries of creation, fall, incarnation, and redemption. In Julian's day, women were officially forbidden to be theological teachers. Yet, after momentarily mistaking her visions for disease-induced "ravings," Julian and others became convinced that they were of divine origin, and that she had a duty, out of love of God and her fellow Christians, to share them. Her writing is poetic and creative, yet deeply indebted to Scripture (especially wisdom traditions and the Gospel of John) and Catholic theology and piety.

The *leitmotif* of Julian's revelations is the depth, breadth, and intimacy of God's love. Julian communicates this "homely," familiar, and "magnificently courteous" love through a rich variety of images. She says: "I saw that he is to us everything that is good and comfortable for us. He is our clothing that for love wraps us, clasps us, and completely encloses us for tender love, that he may never leave us, being to us all things good . . . ." God is present in every creature as "maker, lover, and keeper." Suffusing her theology is Julian's trusting and hopeful encounter with the Divine Trinity as Goodness, whose properties are Life—"marvelous homeliness,", Love—"gentle courtesy," and Light—"endless kindness" (*Revelations*, Ch. 83).

Our Selection: The Trinity and Jesus as "Mother"

The author of the *Revelations* was a devout woman steeped in the affective spirituality of her day. Her prayer-life focused tenderly on Jesus' humanity and sufferings for our sake. She may well have been familiar with Anselm of Canterbury's imaging of Christ giving humankind new birth by his death on the cross, his sufferings like spiritual labor-pains. This late-medieval piety was a congenial context for Julian's contemplation of the motherhood of God. Echoing biblical motifs [Hosea, Paul], Julian speaks passionately of God as our true and faithful husband, and we his "loved wife and sweetheart." Originally developing Anselm's birthing imagery, she calls Jesus our mother, as well as brother and savior.

In the following excerpt, Julian speaks of the mystery of the Trinity and God's relations with humanity. God's *almighty power* is encompassed in the first Person, whose distinguishing attribute is fatherhood. God's *deep wisdom* (recall Proverbs 8) is the second Person—Jesus Christ, whose attribute is motherhood. God's *great love and goodness* overflows as the third Person—the Holy Spirit, whose attribute is empowering and serving lordship. Throughout each stage of our life, God works, dynamically and wonderfully, to bestow nature, mercy, and grace. In our Father, God almighty, we have our being. In our "merciful Mother," Jesus Christ, we have reformation and renewal. In yielding to the gracious and generous impulse of the Holy Spirit we are made perfect. Why is Jesus Christ called Mother? Because "we owe our being to him—this is the essence of mother-hood!" In creation, he gives us our sensual nature. He is also mother to us in grace, as the one through whom we are reborn to new life in God's kingdom. ". . . [H]e, All-love, bears us to joy and eternal life! . . . Thus he carries us within himself in love. . . ." Our beloved Mother, Jesus, feeds us with himself in the sacraments. And like a good mother, Jesus adjusts his methods of teaching to the stages of our growth. So, Julian reiterates, "God is as really our Mother as he is our Father." In her visions, God declares: "[I]t is I who am the strength and goodness of Fatherhood; I who am the wisdom of Moth-erhood; I who am the light and grace of blessed love . . . I who enable you to love; I who enable you to long. It is I, the eternal satisfaction of every genuine desire" (Compare to Augustine, *Confessions,* Book 8).

Mysticism's Aim: Loving Union with God

Authentic Christian mysticism is always embedded in the living reli-gious community of the church. It is a process or way of life whose defining note is the experience of deep union with the divine. As the gifted experience of divine mystery, it is a potential aspect of every Christian's life. In a more intense sense, mysticism is "the graced transformation of consciousness that follows upon a direct or imme-diate experience of the presence of God leading to deeper union with God" (R. McBrien, *Catholicism,* 1052). It was for this intense mysti-cal union or "oneing" that Julian longed. By God's "magnificent courtesy" and "homely love," she experienced this union through her near-death visions, through subsequent years of prayer and reflection, in her inspiration to share her "showings" with all her beloved fellow-Christians.

As for the ultimate meaning of her revelations, Julian wrote later in life:

". . . I desired often to understand *what was our Lord's meaning.* And fifteen years after, and more, I was answered in spiritual understanding:

'Would you know your Lord's meaning in this thing?

Know it well: *Love was his meaning.*

Who showed it to you? *Love.*

What did he show you? *Love.*

For what purpose did he show it? For *love. . . .*' Thus was I taught that Love was our Lord's meaning" (Ch. 86).

The full text of *The Revelations of Divine Love* is available on the internet:

http://www.ccel.org/j/julian/revelations

— *Dr. Christine Firer Hinze*

TEXT

58

God the blessed Trinity is everlasting Being. Just as he is eternal, without beginning, so has his purpose been eternal, namely to make mankind. This fine nature was prepared in the first instance for his own Son, the Second Person. And when he so willed, with the con-

5 currence of each Person of the Trinity, he made all of us at one and the same time. When he made us he joined and united us to himself. By such union we are kept as pure and noble as when we were first made. It is because of this most precious union that we can love our Maker, please him and praise him, thank him and rejoice in him for

10 ever. And this is the plan continually at work in every soul to be saved—the divine will that I have already mentioned. So when he made us God almighty was our kindly Father, and God all-wise our kindly Mother, and the Holy Spirit their love and goodness; all one God, one Lord. In this uniting together he is our real, true husband,

and we his loved wife and sweetheart. He is never displeased with his 15
wife! 'I love you and you love me,' he says, 'and our love will never be
broken.'

I saw the blessed Trinity working. I saw that there were these three
attributes: fatherhood, motherhood, and lordship all in one God. In
the almighty Father we have been sustained and blessed with regard 20
to our created natural being from before all time. By the skill and wisdom of the Second Person we are sustained, restored, and saved with
regard to our sensual nature, for he is our Mother, Brother, and Savior. In our good Lord the Holy Spirit we have, after our life and
hardship is over, that reward and rest which surpasses for ever any and 25
everything we can possibly desire—such is his abounding grace and
magnificent courtesy.

Our life too is threefold. In the first stage we have our being, in the
second our growth, and in the third our perfection. The first is
nature, the second mercy, and the third grace. For the first I realized 30
that the great power of the Trinity is our Father, the deep wisdom our
Mother, and the great love our Lord. All: his we have by nature and
in our created and essential being. Moreover I saw that the Second
Person who is our Mother with regard to our essential nature, that
same dear Person has become our Mother in the matter of our sen- 35
sual nature. We are God's creation twice: essential being and sensual
nature. Our being is that higher part which we have in our Father,
God almighty, and the second Person of the Trinity is Mother of this
basic nature, providing the substance in which we are rooted and
grounded. But he is our Mother also in mercy, since he has taken our 40
sensual nature upon himself. Thus 'our Mother' describes the different ways in which he works, ways which are separate to us, but held
together in him. In our Mother, Christ, we grow and develop; in his
mercy he reforms and restores us; through his passion, death, and resurrection he has united us to our being. So does our Mother work in 45
mercy for all his children who respond to him and obey him.

Grace works with mercy too, and especially in two ways. The work
is that of the Third Person, the Holy Spirit, who works by *rewarding*
and *giving*. Rewarding is the generous gift of truth that the Lord

50   makes to him who has suffered. Giving is a magnanimous gesture
which he makes freely by his grace: perfect, and far beyond the deserts
of any of his creatures.

Thus in our Father, God almighty, we have our being. In our merciful Mother we have reformation and renewal, and our separate parts
55   are integrated into perfect man. In yielding to the gracious impulse of
the Holy Spirit we are made perfect. Our essence is in our Father,
God almighty, and in our Mother, God all-wise, and in our Lord the
Holy Spirit, God all-good. Our essential nature is entire in each Person of the Trinity, who is one God. Our sensual nature is in the
60   Second Person alone, Jesus Christ. In him is the Father too, and the
Holy Spirit. In and by him have we been taken out of hell with a
strong arm; and out of earth's wretchedness have been wonderfully
raised to heaven, and united, most blessedly, to him who is our true
being. And we have developed in spiritual wealth and character
65   through all Christ's virtues, and by the gracious work of the Holy
Spirit.

59

All this blessedness is ours through mercy and grace. We would never
have had it or known it if goodness (that is, God) had not been
opposed. It is because of this that we enjoy this bliss. Wickedness was
70   allowed to rise up against goodness, and the goodness of mercy and
grace rose up against wickedness and then turned it all into goodness
and honor, at least as far as those who are to be saved are concerned.
For it is the way of God to set good against evil. So Jesus Christ who
sets good against evil is our real Mother. We owe our being to him—
75   and this is the essence of motherhood!—and all the delightful, loving
protection which ever follows. God is as really our Mother as he is our
Father. He showed this throughout, and particularly when he said
that sweet word, 'It is I.' In other words, 'It is I who am the strength
and goodness of Fatherhood; I who am the wisdom of Motherhood;
80   I who am light and grace and blessed love; I who am Trinity; I who
am Unity; I who am the sovereign goodness of every single thing; I

who enable you to love; I who enable you to long. It is I the eternal satisfaction of every genuine desire.'

For the soul is at its best, its most noble and honorable, when it is most lowly, and humble, and gentle. Springing from this fundamental source and as part of our natural endowment, are all the virtues of our sensual nature, aided and abetted as they are by mercy and grace. Without such assistance we should be in a poor way!

Our great Father, God almighty, who is Being, knew and loved us from eternity. Through his knowledge, and in the marvellous depths of his charity, together with the foresight and wisdom of the whole blessed Trinity, he willed that the Second Person should become our Mother, Brother, and Savior. Hence it follows that God is as truly our Mother as he is our Father. Our Father decides, our Mother works, our good Lord, the Holy Spirit, strengthens. So we ought to love our God in whom we have our own being, reverently thanking him, and praising him for creating us, earnestly beseeching our Mother for mercy and pity, and our Lord, the Spirit, for help and grace. For in these three is contained our life: nature, mercy, grace. From these we get our humility, gentleness, patience and pity. From them too we get our hatred of sin and wickedness—it is the function of virtue to hate these.

So we see that Jesus is the true Mother of our nature, for he made us. He is our Mother, too, by grace, because he took our created nature upon himself. All the lovely deeds and tender services that beloved motherhood implies are appropriate to the Second Person. In him the godly will is always safe and sound, both in nature and grace, because of his own fundamental goodness. I came to realize that there were three ways of looking at God's motherhood: the first is based on the fact that our nature is *made;* the second is found in the assumption of that nature—there begins the motherhood of grace; the third is the motherhood of work which flows out over all by that same grace—the length and breadth and height and depth of it is everlasting. And so is his love.

60

115 But now I must say a little more about this 'over-flowing' as I understand its meaning: how we have been brought back again by the
motherhood of mercy and grace to that natural condition which was
ours originally when we were made through the motherhood of natural love which love, indeed, has never left us.

120 Our Mother by nature and grace—for he would become our
Mother in everything—laid the foundation of his work in the Virgin's
womb with great and gentle condescension. (This was shown in the
first revelation when I received a mental picture of the Virgin's genuine simplicity at the time she conceived.) In other words, it was in

125 this lowly place that God most high, the supreme wisdom of all,
adorned and arrayed himself with our poor flesh, ready to function
and serve as Mother in all things.

A mother's is the most intimate, willing, and dependable of all services, because it is the truest of all. None has been able to fulfil it

130 properly but Christ, and he alone can. We know that our own
mother's bearing of us was a bearing to pain and death, but what does
Jesus, our true Mother, do? Why, he, All-love, bears us to joy and eternal life! Blessings on him! Thus he carries us within himself in love.
And he is in labor until the time has fully come for him to suffer the

135 sharpest pangs and most appalling pain possible—and in the end he
dies. And not even when this is over, and we ourselves have been born
to eternal bliss, is his marvellous love completely satisfied. This he
shows in that overwhelming word of love, 'If I could possibly have
suffered more, indeed I would have done so.'

140 He might die no more, but that does not stop him working, for he
needs to feed us. . .it is an obligation of his dear, motherly, love. The
human mother will suckle her child with her own milk, but our
beloved Mother, Jesus feeds us with himself, and, with the most tender courtesy, does it by means of the Blessed Sacrament, the precious

145 food of all true life. And he keeps us going through his mercy and
grace by all the sacraments. This is what he meant when he said, 'It is
I whom Holy Church preaches and teaches.' In other words, 'All the

health and life of sacraments, all the virtue and grace of my word, all the goodness laid up for you in Holy Church—it is I.' The human mother may put her child tenderly to her breast, but our tender 150 Mother Jesus simply leads us into his blessed breast through his open side, and there gives us a glimpse of the Godhead and heavenly joy— the inner certainty of eternal bliss. The tenth revelation showed this, and said as much with that word, 'See how I love you', as looking into his side he rejoiced. 155

This fine and lovely word *Mother* is so sweet and so much its own that it cannot properly be used of any but him, and of her who is his own true Mother—and ours. In essence *motherhood* means love and kindness, wisdom, knowledge, goodness. Though in comparison with our spiritual birth our physical birth is a small, unimportant, straight- 160 forward sort of thing, it still remains that it is only through his working that it can be done at all by his creatures. A kind, loving mother who understands and knows the needs of her child will look after it tenderly just because it is the nature of a mother to do so. As the child grows older she changes her methods—but not her love. 165 Older still, she allows the child to be punished so that its faults are corrected and its virtues and graces developed. This way of doing things, with much else that is right and good, is our Lord at work in those who are doing them. Thus he is our Mother in nature, working by his grace in our lower part, for the sake of the higher. It is his will 170 that we should know this, for he wants all our love to be fastened on himself. Like this I could see that our indebtedness, under God, to fatherhood and motherhood—whether it be human or divine—is fully met in truly loving God. And this blessed love Christ himself produces in us. This was shown in all the revelations, and especially 175 in those splendid words that he uttered, 'It is I whom you love.'

15

"On Christian Freedom"
(An Excerpt)

MARTIN LUTHER (1483–1546)

INTRODUCTION

This 1520 treatise is a devotional booklet to accompany Martin Luther's conciliatory Open Letter to Pope Leo X. Prominent themes are freedom and servanthood, based on Luther's fundamental distinction between law and Gospel. Law is a code-word for any attempt to reach heaven by human effort outside of Christ. Either Christ saves completely or not at all. The Gospel is the word of forgiveness.

The medieval pilgrim is beset with law on all sides: the church's penitential system, scholastic theology, monastic vows. Law enslaves; Gospel frees.

1. Freedom

A Christian is freed by the Gospel from works of the law. Works do not save; only Christ does. The soul is justified by faith alone. The inward man becomes righteous and free through the holy Word of God received in faith.

The commands of the law lead only to despair of our inability to fulfill them. The promise of the Gospel brings peace and fulfillment of the law through faith in Christ.

The first power of faith is Christian freedom, our faith. The second power is to cling to the promise and obey God in all things. The third benefit of faith is that the soul is united to Christ as the bride with her bridegroom. In one flesh the sins of the bride are swallowed up in Christ.

One with Christ we are all priests worthy to appear before God in prayer. Though we cannot all publicly minister and teach, as co-heirs with Christ we may boldly come into the presence of God in prayer. A terrible tyranny of power among ecclesiastics has perverted Christian grace, faith, and freedom.

2. Servanthood

A Christian is a servant to the neighbor as Christ took on the form of a servant. The outward man must govern his own body and have dealings with other people. Here the works begin. He must discipline the body so that it will obey and conform to the inward man of faith. Though not justifying, the good works purify the body of evil lusts. Good works are spontaneous love of the neighbor in obedience to God.

The purpose of good works is not salvation but the need of the neighbor. Works of love issue in free service to others without regard for reward. The Christian gives of himself as a Christ to the neighbor. From faith flows a loving and joyful person freely serving the neighbor, taking no account of gratitude, praise, or gain. We are to be Christs to one another.

A Christian lives in Christ through faith and in the neighbor through love. Christian freedom makes our hearts free from all sins, laws, and mandates.

— Dr. Kenneth G. Hagen

TEXT

A Treatise on Christian Liberty (1520)

A Christian man is a perfectly free lord of all, subject to none.
A Christian man is a perfectly dutiful servant of all, subject to all.

Although these two theses seem to contradict each other, yet, if they should be found to fit together they would serve our purpose beautifully. For they are both Paul's own, who says, in I Cor. 9, "Whereas I was free, I made myself the servant of all," and, Rom. 13, "Owe no man anything, but to love one another." Now love by its very nature is ready to serve and to be subject to him who is loved. So, Christ, although Lord of all, was made of a woman, made under the law, and hence was at the same time free and a servant, at the same time in the form of God and in the form of a servant.

Let us start, however, with something more obvious. Man has a twofold nature, a spiritual and a bodily, [and these two] contradict each other, since the flesh lusteth against the spirit and the spirit against the flesh (Gal. 5).

First, let us contemplate the inward man, to see how a righteous, free and truly Christian man, that is, a new, spiritual, inward man, comes into being. It is evident that no external thing, whatsoever it be, has any influence whatever in producing Christian righteousness or liberty, nor in producing unrighteousness or bondage. A simple argument will furnish the proof. What can it profit the soul if the body fare well, be free and active, eat, drink and do as it pleases? For in these things even the most godless slaves of all the vices fare well. On the other hand, how will ill health or imprisonment or hunger or thirst or any other external misfortune hurt the soul? With these things even the most godly men are afflicted, and those who because of a clear conscience are most free. None of these things touch either the liberty or the bondage of the soul. The soul receives no benefit if the body is adorned with the sacred robes of the priesthood, or dwells in sacred places, or is occupied with sacred duties, or prays, fasts, abstains from certain kinds of food or does any work whatsoever that

5

10

15

20

25

30

can be done by the body and in the body. . . . On the other hand, it will not hurt the soul if the body is clothed in secular dress, dwells in unconsecrated places, eats and drinks as others do, does not pray

35 aloud, and neglects to do all the things mentioned above, which hypocrites can do.

One thing and one only is necessary for Christian life, righteousness and liberty. That one thing is the most holy Word of God, the Gospel of Christ . . . You ask, "What then is this Word of God, and

40 how shall it be used, since there are so many words of God?" I answer, The Apostle explains that in Romans 1. The Word is the Gospel of God concerning his Son, Who was made flesh, suffered, rose from the dead, and was glorified through the Spirit Who sanctifies. For to preach Christ means to feed the soul, to make it righteous, to set it

45 free and to save it, if it believes the preaching. For faith alone is the saving and efficacious use of the Word of God, Romans 10, "If thou confess with thy mouth that Jesus is Lord, and believe with thy heart that God hath raised Him up from the dead, thou shalt be saved"; and again, "The end of the law is Christ, unto righteousness to every

50 one that believeth"; and, Romans 1, "The just shall live by his faith." The Word of God cannot be received and cherished by any works whatever, but only by faith. Hence it is clear that, as the soul needs only the Word for its life and righteousness, so it is justified by faith alone and not by any works; for if it could be justified by anything

55 else, it would not need the Word, and therefore it would not need faith. But this faith cannot at all exist in connection with works, that is to say, if you at the same time claim to be justified by works, whatever their character; for that would be to halt between two sides, to worship Baal and to kiss the hand, which, as Job says, is a very great

60 iniquity. . . . When you have learned this, you will know that you need Christ, Who suffered and rose again for you, that, believing in Him, you may through this faith become a new man, in that all your sins are forgiven, and you are justified by the merits of another, namely, of Christ alone.

Since, therefore, this faith can rule only in the inward man, as 65
Romans 10 says, "With the heart we believe unto righteousness"; and
since faith alone justifies, it is clear that the inward man cannot be
justified, made free and be saved by any outward work or dealing
whatsoever, and that works, whatever their character, have nothing to
do with this inward man. . . . Wherefore it ought to be the first con- 70
cern of every Christian to lay aside all trust in works, and more and
more to strengthen faith alone, and through faith to grow in the
knowledge, not of works, but of Christ Jesus.

Should you ask, how it comes that faith alone justifies and without
works offers us such a treasury of great benefits, when so many works, 75
ceremonies and laws are prescribed in the Scriptures, I answer: First
of all, remember what has been said: faith alone, without works, justifies, makes free and saves, as we shall later make still more clear.
Here we must point out that all the Scriptures of God are divided into
two parts—commands and promises. The commands indeed teach 80
things that are good, but the things taught are not done as soon as
taught; for the commands show us what we ought to do, but do not
give us the power to do it; they are intended to teach a man to know
himself, that through them he may recognize his inability to do good
and may despair of his powers. That is why they are called and are the 85
Old Testament. . . .

But when a man through the commands has learned to know his
weakness, and has become troubled as to how he may satisfy the law,
since the law must be fulfilled so that not a jot or tittle shall perish,
otherwise man will be condemned without hope; then, being truly 90
humbled and reduced to nothing in his own eyes, he finds in himself
no means of justification and salvation. Here the second part of the
Scriptures stands ready—the promises of God, which declare the
glory of God and say, "If you wish to fulfil the law, and not to covet,
as the law demands, come, believe in Christ, in Whom grace, right- 95
eousness, peace, liberty and all things are promised you; if you believe
you shall have all, if you believe not you shall lack all." For what is

impossible for you in all the works of the law, many as they are, but all useless, you will accomplish in a short and easy way through faith.
100 For God our Father has made all things depend on faith, so that whoever has faith, shall have all, and whoever has it not, shall have nothing. "For He has concluded all under unbelief, that He might have mercy on all," Romans 11. Thus the promises of God give what the commands of God ask, and fulfil what the law prescribes, that all
105 things may be of God alone, both the commands and the fulfilling of the commands. He alone commands, He also alone fulfils. Therefore the promises of God belong to the New Testament, nay, they are the New Testament. . . .

No work can cling to the Word of God nor be in the soul; in the
110 soul faith alone and the Word have sway. As the Word is, so it makes the soul, as heated iron glows like fire because of the union of fire with it. It is clear then that a Christian man has in his faith all that he needs, and needs no works to justify him. And if he has no need of works, neither does he need the law; and if he has no need of the law,
115 surely he is free from the law, and it is true, "The law is not made for a righteous man." And this is that Christian liberty, even our faith, which does not indeed cause us to live in idleness or in wickedness, but makes the law and works unnecessary for any man's righteousness and salvation.

120 This is the first power of faith. Let us now examine the second also. For it is a further function of faith, that whom it trusts it also honors with the most reverent and high regard, since it considers him truthful and trustworthy. . . . So when the soul firmly trusts God's promises, it regards Him as truthful and righteous, than which noth-
125 ing more excellent can be ascribed to God. This is the very highest worship of God. . . Then the soul consents to all His will, then it hallows His name and suffers itself to be dealt with according to God's good pleasure, because, clinging to God's promises, it does not doubt that He, Who is true, just and wise, will do, dispose and provide all
130 things well. And is not such a soul, by this faith, in all things most obedient to God? . . .

The third incomparable benefit of faith is this, that it unites the soul with Christ as a bride is united with her bridegroom. And by this mystery, as the Apostle teaches, Christ and the soul become one flesh. . . .   135

Who can fully appreciate what this royal marriage means? Who can understand the riches of the glory of this grace? Here this rich and godly Bridegroom Christ marries this poor, wicked harlot, redeems her from all her evil and adorns her with all His good. It is now impossible that her sins should destroy her, since they are laid upon   140 Christ and swallowed up in Him, and she has that righteousness in Christ her husband of which she may boast as of her own, and which she can confidently set against all her sins in the face of death and hell. . . .

Just as Christ by his birthright obtained these two prerogatives   145 (priesthood and kingship), so He imparts them to and shares them with every one who believes on Him according to the law of the aforesaid marriage, by which the wife owns whatever belongs to the husband. Hence we are all priests and kings in Christ, as many as believe on Christ, as I Pet. 2 says, "Ye are a chosen generation, a pecu-   150 liar people, a royal priesthood and priestly kingdom, that ye should show forth the virtues of Him Who hath called you out of darkness into His marvelous light . . ."

Not only are we the freest of kings, we are also priests forever, which is far more excellent than being kings, because as priests we are   155 worthy to appear before God to pray for others and to teach one another the things of God. For these are the functions of priests, and cannot be granted to any unbeliever. Thus Christ has obtained for us, if we believe on Him, that we are not only His brethren, co-heirs and fellow-kings with Him, but also fellow-priests with Him, who may   160 boldly come into the presence of God in the spirit of faith. . . .

A Christian man is free from all things and over all things, so that he needs no works to make him righteous and to save him, since faith alone confers all these abundantly. But should he grow so foolish as to presume to become righteous by means of some good work, he   165 would on the instant lose faith and all its benefits: a foolishness aptly illustrated in the fable of the dog who runs along a stream with a piece of meat in his mouth, and, deceived by the reflection of the meat in the water, opens his mouth to snap at it, so loses both the meat and 170 the reflection.

You will ask, "If all who are in the Church are priests, how do those whom we now call priests differ from laymen?" I answer: "Injustice is done those words, 'priest,' 'cleric,' 'spiritual,' 'ecclesiastic,' when they are transferred from all other Christians to those few who are now by 175 a mischievous usage called 'ecclesiastics.' For Holy Scripture makes no distinction between them, except that it gives the name 'ministers,' 'servants,' 'stewards,' to those who are now proudly called popes, bishops, and lords and who should by the ministry of the Word serve others and teach them the faith of Christ and the liberty of believers. 180 For although we are all equally priests, yet we cannot all publicly minister and teach, nor ought we if we could."

But that stewardship has now been developed into so great a pomp of power and so terrible a tyranny, that no heathen empire or earthly power can be compared with it, just as if laymen were not also Chris- 185 tians. Through this perversion the knowledge of Christian grace, faith, liberty and of Christ himself has altogether perished, and its place has been taken by an unbearable bondage of human words and laws. . . .

Now let us turn to the second part, to the outward man. Here we 190 shall answer all those who, misled by the word "faith" and by all that has been said, now say: "If faith does all things and is alone sufficient unto righteousness, why then are good works commanded? We will take our ease and do no works, and be content with faith." I answer, Not so, ye wicked men, not so. That would indeed be proper, if we 195 were wholly inward and perfectly spiritual men; but such we shall be only at the last day, the day of the resurrection of the dead. As long as we live in the flesh we only begin and make some progress in that which shall be perfected in the future life. . . .

Although, as I have said, a man is abundantly justified by faith inwardly, in his spirit, and so has all that he ought to have, except in so far as this faith and riches must grow from day to day even unto the future life: yet he remains in this mortal life on earth, and in this life he must needs govern his own body and have dealings with men. Here the works begin; here a man cannot take his ease; here he must, indeed, take care to discipline his body by fastings, watchings, labors and other reasonable discipline, and to make it subject to the spirit so that it will obey and conform to the inward man and to faith, and not revolt against faith and hinder the inward man, as it is the body's nature to do if it be not held in check. For the inward man, who by faith is created in the likeness of God, is both joyful and happy because of Christ in Whom so many benefits are conferred upon him, and therefore it is his one occupation to serve God joyfully and for naught, in love that is not constrained.

In doing these works, however, we must not think that a man is justified before God by them: for that erroneous opinion faith, which alone is righteousness before God, cannot endure; but we must think that these works reduce the body to subjection and purify it of its evil lusts, and our whole purpose is to be directed only toward the driving out of lusts. For since by faith the soul is cleansed and made a lover of God, it desires that all things, and especially its own body, shall be as pure as itself, so that all things may join with it in loving and praising God. Hence a man cannot be idle, because the need of his body drives him and he is compelled to do many good works to reduce it to subjection. Nevertheless the works themselves do not justify him before God, but he does the works out of spontaneous love in obedience to God, and considers nothing except the approval of God, Whom he would in all things most scrupulously obey.

In this way every one will easily be able to learn for himself the limit and discretion, as they say, of his bodily castigations: for he will fast, watch and labor as much as he finds sufficient to repress the lasciviousness and lust of his body. But they who presume to be justified

235   by works do not regard the mortifying of the lusts, but only the works themselves, and think that if only they have done as many and as great works as are possible, they have done well, and have become righteousness; at times they even addle their brains and destroy, or at least render useless, their natural strength with their works. This is the height of folly, and utter ignorance of Christian life and faith, that a man should seek to be justified and saved by works and without faith.

* * *

240   But none of these things does a man need for his righteousness and salvation. Therefore, in all his works he should be guided by this thought and look to this one thing alone, that he may serve and benefit others in all that he does, having regard to nothing except the need and the advantage of his neighbor. Thus, the Apostle commands us to work with our hands that we may give to him who is in need,
245   although he might have said that we should work to support ourselves. And this is what makes it a Christian work to care for the body, that through its health and comfort we may be able to work, to acquire and to lay by funds with which to aid those who are in need, that in this way the strong member may serve the weaker, and we may
250   be sons of God, each caring for and working for the other, bearing one another's burdens, and so fulfilling the law of Christ. Lo, this is a truly Christian life, here faith is truly effectual through love; that is, it issues in works of the freest service cheerfully and lovingly done, with which a man willingly serves another without hope of
255   reward, and for himself is satisfied with the fullness and wealth of his faith. . . .

Although the Christian is thus free from all works, he ought in this liberty to empty himself, to take upon himself the form of a servant, to be made in the likeness of men, to be found in fashion as a man,
260   and to serve, help and in every way deal with his neighbor as he sees that God through Christ has dealt and still deals with himself. And this he should do freely, having regard to nothing except the divine approval. He ought to think: "Though I am an unworthy and con-

demned man, my God has given me in Christ all the riches of righteousness and salvation without any merit on my part, out of pure,   265
free mercy, so that henceforth I need nothing whatever except faith
which believes that this is true. Why should I not therefore freely, joyfully, with all my heart, and with an eager will, do all things which I
know are pleasing and acceptable to such a Father, Who has over-
whelmed with His inestimable riches? I will therefore give myself as a   270
Christ to my neighbor, just as Christ offered Himself to me; I will do
nothing in this life except what I see is necessary, profitable and salutary to my neighbor, since through faith I have an abundance of all
good things in Christ."

Lo, thus from faith flow forth love and joy in the Lord, and from   275
love a joyful, willing and free mind that serves one's neighbor willingly and takes no account of gratitude or ingratitude, of praise or
blame, of gain or loss. For a man does not serve that he may put men
under obligations, he does not distinguish between friends and enemies, nor does he anticipate their thankfulness or unthankfulness; but   280
most freely and most willingly he spends himself and all that he has,
whether he waste all on the thankless or whether he gain a reward. For
as his Father does, distributing all things to all men richly and freely,
causing His sun to rise upon the good and upon the evil, so also the
son does all things and suffers all things with that freely bestowing joy   285
which is his delight when through Christ he sees it in God, the dis-
penser of such great benefits.

Therefore, if we recognize the great and precious things which are
given us, as Paul says, there will be shed abroad in our hearts by the
Holy Ghost the love which makes us free, joyful, almighty workers   290
and conquerors over all tribulations, servants of our neighbors and yet
lords of all. But for those who do not recognize the gifts bestowed
upon them through Christ, Christ has been born in vain; they go
their way with their works, and shall never come to taste or to feel
those things. Just as our neighbor is in need and lacks that in which   295
we abound, so we also have been in need before God and have lacked
His mercy. Hence, as our heavenly Father has in Christ freely come

300   to our help, we also ought freely to help our neighbor through our body and its works, and each should become as it were a Christ to the other, that we may be Christs to one another and Christ may be the same in all; that is, that we may be truly Christians.

* * *

305   We conclude, therefore, that a Christian man lives not in himself, but in Christ and in his neighbor. Otherwise he is not a Christian. He lives in Christ through faith, in his neighbor through love; by faith he is caught beyond himself into God, by love he sinks down beneath himself into his neighbor; yet he always remains in God and in His love.

310   Liberty is spiritual, and makes our hearts free from all sins, laws and mandates. This liberty may Christ grant us both to understand and to preserve. Amen.

16

Autobiography (An Excerpt)

IGNATIUS OF LOYOLA (1491–1556)

INTRODUCTION

In an autobiography someone tells the story of his or her own life, often because the author has done something conspicuous. Although others may know something of his or her public deeds and words, an autobiography allows the person to relate interior motives and personal perspectives behind visible deeds.

St. Ignatius Loyola (1491–1556) is a canonized saint in the Catholic Church. The term "saint" refers to a holy man or woman whom the Church officially holds as an example and as one who can intercede with God for all of us. The term derives from the same Latin root (*sacer*=sacred) as sanctify, which means "to make holy." Jesus the Christ teaches, governs and sanctifies the faithful in and through the preaching of the gospel, the celebration of the Church's liturgy, and the invisible work of grace. Saints are those in whom this ministry of Christ has come to its fullest effect.

Chapter One of the *Autobiography* makes it plain that the young Ignatius was a fiery leader, but otherwise an ordinary, sinful human being until something happened in 1521. This event had an external and public aspect: a soldier wounded in battle and then recuperating at home. It had an internal aspect as well.

Chapter One gives us a detailed description of how daydreams, stimulated by books supplied to him during the healing of his leg, began Ignatius' journey to God. He read, first from books of love stories involving gallant deeds—a kind of the soap opera of the time, then from lives of Christ and the saints, then back to the stories. Fantasizing alternately on both types of stories, he noticed a difference in moods generated by each type of reading. Deep peace after reading about Christ and the saints drew him to imitate the sacrifices they made, whereas the chivalrous feats of medieval knights afterwards left his spirit empty and dry. From that awakening to his own interior life there gradually resulted a new consciousness and life in the Spirit, marked by a particular way of helping other people hear and live the gospel.

In 1522 Ignatius began a pilgrimage to the Holy Land but delayed for ten months of prayer, living in a cave at Manresa, some miles west of Barcelona. When he returned from his journey to the holy sites, he devoted himself to academic studies: three years in Spain and seven more at the University of Paris. In Spain he was detained and questioned by the Inquisition because, until he eventually finished studying theology at Paris, he was teaching others about God's ways as a layman without the solid benefit of theology, though he had divine guidance.

Ignatius is widely known through history as the founder of the Society of Jesus, the Jesuits. During his student days in Paris he attracted student-companions who also wanted to devote themselves to God. He guided them, one at a time, through a month-long prayer experience according to notes he took during his own ten months of prayer in Manresa, notes which came to be known as the *Spiritual Exercises*. Out of that nucleus of men, formed by those exercises, there emerged a new religious congregation. Religious here is a term referring to that kind of *imitatio Christi* (imitation of Christ) in the Church organized by vows of poverty, chastity, and obedience for the purpose of promoting personal union with God in oneself and in others. In the perspective of Catholic faith, marriage and religious life are complementary, not antithetical, routes toward the same goal of loving God above all things and one's neighbor as oneself–sharing in Christ's mission to the world.

—Rev. D. Thomas Hughson, S.J.

TEXT[1]

**The Life of Father Ignatius
as first written by Father Luis González
who received it from the lips of
the Father himself.**

Author's Preface

1   One Friday morning of the year 1553, it being August 4th and the eve of Our Lady of the Snows, the Father was standing in the garden near the house or the room which is called the Duke's, when I began to give him an account of some of the particulars of my soul. Among other things, I spoke to him of vainglory. The Father suggested as remedy the frequent referring of all my affairs to God, making a serious effort to offer Him all the good there was in me, recognizing it as belonging to Him, and giving Him thanks for it. He spoke in a way that consoled me very much, so that I could not hold back my tears. The Father related to me how he had struggled against this vice for two years, to the extent that when he took ship in Barcelona bound for Jerusalem, he did not dare tell anybody that he was going to Jerusalem.[2] He acted the same way in other particulars, and, what is more, he added that he had enjoyed great peace of soul on this point ever afterwards. An hour or two after this we went to

5

10

15

---

[1] Translated by William J. Young, S.J.

[2] His reluctance to speak of his Jerusalem pilgrimage was due to the distinction attached at the time to such pilgrims. He was anxious to avoid every occasion of self-complacence.

table, and while Master Polanco[3] and I were eating, our Father told me that Master Nadal[4] and others of the Society had often made a request of him, but that he had never made up his mind about it; but that after he had spoken with me, thinking the matter over in his
20 room, he felt a great inclination and devotion to do so. He spoke in such a way as to show that God had greatly enlightened him about his duty so to do, and that he had for once and all made up his mind. That request was to make known all that had taken place in his soul up to that moment. He had also decided that it was I to whom he was
25 going to make these things known.

2   At that time, the Father was in very bad health, and was not accustomed to promise himself life from one day to the next. In fact, when he heard anyone saying, "I will do this two weeks from now, or a week from now," the Father was always a bit amazed: "How's that?
30 Do you count on living that long?" And yet, on this occasion, he said that he hoped to live three or four months so as to bring this matter to an end. The other day I spoke to him and asked him when he wished to begin. He answered that I should remind him every day (I don't remember how many) until he was ready. But as business pre-
35 vented him he had me remind him of it every Sunday. It was then in September (I don't recall the day), that the Father called me and began the narrative of his whole life, recounting his youthful excesses clearly and distinctly with all their circumstances. Later in the same month he called me three or four times, and carried his story up to
40 within a few days of his stay at Manresa, as will be seen in the part written by a different hand.

3   The Father's way of telling his story is what he uses in all things. It is done with such clearness that it makes the whole past pre-

---

[3] A Spanish Jesuit, probably from a family of Jewish converts to Christianity, Fr. Juan Alfonso de Polanco was secretary to Ignatius in the saint's capacity as General superior of the Society of Jesus.

[4] Fr. Jerónimo Nadal, a native of Majorca and another assistant to Ignatius, was a brilliant theologian and the finest interpreter of Ignatius' mind to the rest of the Society of Jesus.

sent to the beholder. There was no need, therefore, of putting any questions, for the Father remembered and told whatever was worth knowing. I went at once to write it out, without a word to the Father, first in notes in my own hand, and later at greater length as it now stands. I have taken pains not to insert any word that I did not hear from our Father, and if there is anything in which I am afraid of having failed, it is that by not wishing to depart from the words of the Father, I have not been able to explain clearly the meaning of some of them. I kept writing in this way until September of 1553, as I have said. But from then on, after the arrival of Father Nadal, October 18, 1554, the Father constantly kept excusing himself because of some illness or the various engagements which turned up, saying, "When this matter is finished, remind me"; and when that was finished, he kept saying, "Now we are busy with this. When it is finished, remind me."

4   When Father Nadal arrived, he was delighted to find that we had begun, and bade me importune the Father, often telling me that the Father could in nothing do more good to the Society [of Jesus] than in this, that this was really to found the Society. He too, therefore, frequently spoke to the Father, and the Father told me that I should remind him when they finished the business of the endowment of the college. But when that was finished, he had to go on with the affair of Prester John,[5] and the mail was ready to leave. On the ninths of March we began to take up the history. But at once, Pope Julius became dangerously ill and died the 25th. Then the Father kept putting it off until we had a new pope who, as soon as he was named, also fell ill and died (Marcellus).[6] The Father delayed until the creation of Paul IV,[7] and then, what with the great heat and his numerous occupations, he kept holding off until the 21st of

---

[5] This refers to the plans for a mission to Ethiopia, the emperor of which the Portuguese and others at the time thought was the famous Prester John.

[6] Marcellus II (Cervini) was elected pope April 9, 1555 and died the 30th of the same month.

[7] Paul IV (Pietro Carafa), elected May 23, 1555.

September, when arrangements began to be made for my transfer to
Spain. For these reasons I urged the Father to make good his promise,
and so he arranged for a meeting on the morning of the 22nd in the
75   Red Tower. When I finished Mass I went to him to ask whether it
was time.

He answered me to go and wait for him in the Red Tower,[8] so that
I should be there when he came. I understood that I should have to
wait for him there. But while I was delaying in a passageway, to
80   answer the questions of one of the brethren about some matter of
business, the Father came and reproved me because I had overstepped
the limits of obedience and failed to be waiting for him. He would
do nothing that day. But we brought great pressure to bear upon him.
. . . As a result he returned to the Red Tower and dictated as he
85   walked, as he always did. But I kept drawing a little closer to him so
that I could see his face, and the Father told me to observe the rule.
Growing negligent, I drew near him and fell into the same fault two
or three times. He told me about it and went off. At length he
returned, so that in that same Tower he finished dictating what has
90   been written. But as I was on the point of beginning my journey, the
preceding day being the last on which the Father spoke to me about
this matter, I did not have time to write out everything at length at
Rome. And because I did not have a Spanish secretary at Genoa, I
dictated in Italian the points I had jotted down and brought with me
95   from Rome. This writing I finished at Genoa in December 1555.

Chapter 1

1   Up to his twenty-sixth year he was a man given over to the vanities of the world, and took a special delight in the exercise of arms,
with a great and vain desire of winning glory. He was in a fortress[9]

---

[8] A small dwelling adjoining the professed house at Rome, frequently used as
an infirmary.

[9] The castle of Pamplona.

which the French were attacking, and although the others were of the opinion that they should surrender on terms of having their lives spared, as they clearly saw there as no possibility of a defense, he gave so many reasons to the governor that he persuaded him to carry on the defense against the judgment of the officers, who found some strength in his spirit and courage. On the day on which they expected the attack to take place, he made his confession to one of his companions in arms. After the assault had been going on for some time, a cannon ball struck him in the leg, crushing its bones, and because it passed between his legs it also seriously wounded the other.

2   With his fall, the others in the fortress surrendered to the French, who took possession, and treated the wounded man with great kindliness and courtesy. After twelve or fifteen days in Pamplona they bore him in a litter to his own country. Here he found himself in a very serious condition. The doctors and surgeons whom he had called from all parts were of the opinion that the leg should be operated on again and the bones reset, either because they had been poorly set in the first place, or because the jarring of the journey had displaced them so that they would not heal. Again he went through this butchery, in which as in all the others that he had suffered he uttered no word, nor gave any sign of pain other than clenching his fists.

3   His condition grew worse. Besides being unable to eat he showed other symptoms which are usually a sign of approaching death. The feast of St. John[10] drew near, and as the doctors had very little hope of his recovery, they advised him to make his confession. He received the last sacraments on the eve of the feast of Sts. Peter and Paul,[11] and the doctors told him that if he showed no improvement by midnight, he could consider himself as good as dead. The patient

---

[10] June 24th, the feast of the Birth of St. John the Baptist.

[11] The feast day itself is June 29th.

had some devotion to St. Peter, and so our Lord wished that his improvement should begin that very midnight. So rapid was his recovery that within a few days he was thought to be out of danger of death.

4   When the bones knit, one below the knee remained astride another, which caused a shortening of the leg. The bones so raised caused a protuberance that was not pleasant to the sight. The sick man was not able to put up with this, because he had made up his mind to seek his fortune in the world. He thought the protuberance was going to be unsightly and asked the surgeons whether it could not be cut away. They told him that it could be cut away, but that the pain would be greater than all he had already suffered, because it was now healed and it would take some time to cut if off. He determined, nevertheless, to undergo this martyrdom to gratify his own inclinations. His elder brother was quite alarmed and declared that he would not have the courage to undergo such pain. But the wounded man put up with it with his usual patience.

5   After the superfluous flesh and the bone were cut away, means were employed for preventing the one leg from remaining shorter than the other. Many ointments were applied and devices employed for keeping the leg continually stretched which caused him many days of martyrdom. But it was our Lord Who restored his health. In everything else he was quite well, but he was not able to stand upon that leg, and so had to remain in bed. He had been much given to reading worldly books of fiction and knight errantry, and feeling well enough to read he asked for some of these books to help while away the time. In that house, however, they could find none of those he was accustomed to read, and so they gave him a Life of Christ[12] and a book of the Lives of the Saints in Spanish.

6   By the frequent reading of these books he conceived some affection for what he found there narrated. Pausing in his reading, he

---

[12] By Ludolf of Saxony.

gave himself up to thinking over what he had read. At other times he dwelt on the things of the world which formerly had occupied his thoughts. Of the many vain things that presented themselves to him, one took such possession of his heart that without realizing it he could spend two, three, or even four hours on end thinking of it, fancying what he would have to do in the service of a certain lady, of the means he would take to reach the country where she was living, of the verses, the promises he would make her, the deeds of gallantry he would do in her service. He was so enamored with all this that he did not see how impossible it would all be, because the lady was of no ordinary rank; neither countess, nor duchess, but of a nobility much higher than any of these.[13]

7 Nevertheless, our Lord came to his assistance, for He saw to it that these thoughts were succeeded by others which sprang from the things he was reading. In reading the Life of the Lord and the Lives of the Saints, he paused to think and reason with himself. "Suppose that I should do what St. Francis did, what St. Dominic did?" He thus let his thoughts run over many things that seemed good to him, always putting before himself things that were difficult and important which seemed to him easy to accomplish when he proposed them. But all this thought was to tell himself, "St. Dominic did this, therefore I must do it. St. Francis did this; therefore, I must do it." These thoughts also lasted a good while. And then other things taking their place, the worldly thoughts above mentioned came upon him and remained a long time with him. This succession of diverse thoughts was of long duration, and they were either of worldly achievements which he desired to accomplish, or those of God which took hold of his imagination to such an extent, that worn out with the struggle, he turned them all aside and gave his attention to other things.

---

[13] Who this lady was is not clearly known. From the wording of the Spanish text her station was higher than that of countess or duchess. Some have suggested Queen Germaine, widow of Ferdinand; others, the Princess Catherine, sister of Charles V.

8   There was, however, this difference. When he was thinking of the things of the world he was filled with delight, but when afterwards he dismissed them from weariness, he was dry and dissatisfied. And when he thought of going barefoot to Jerusalem and of eating nothing but herbs and performing the other rigors he saw that the saints had performed, he was consoled, not only when he entertained these thoughts, but even after dismissing them he remained cheerful and satisfied. But he paid no attention to this, nor did he stop to weigh the difference until one day his eyes were opened a little and he began to wonder at the difference and to reflect on it, learning from experience that one kind of thoughts left him sad and the other cheerful. Thus, step by step, he came to recognize the difference between the two spirits that moved him, the one being from the evil spirit, the other from God.

9   He acquired no little light from this reading and began to think more seriously of his past life and the great need he had of doing penance for it. It was during this reading that these desires of imitating the saints came to him, but with no further thought of circumstances than of promising to do with God's grace what they had done. What he desired most of all to do, as soon as he was restored to health, was to go to Jerusalem, as above stated, undertaking all the disciplines and abstinences which a generous soul on fire with the love of God is wont to desire.

10   The thoughts of the past were soon forgotten in the presence of these holy desires, which were confirmed by the following vision. One night, as he lay awake, he saw clearly the likeness of our Lady with the holy Child Jesus, at the sight of which he received most abundant consolation for a considerable interval of time. He felt so great a disgust with his past life, especially with its offenses of the flesh, that he thought all such images which had formerly occupied his mind were wiped out. And from that hour until August of 1553, when this is being written, he never again consented to the least suggestion of the flesh. This effect would seem to indicate that the vision was from God, although he never ventured to affirm it positively, or

claim that it was anything more than he had said it was. But his brother and other members of the family easily recognized the change that had taken place in the interior of his soul from what they saw in his outward manner.   225

11   Without a care in the world he went on with his reading and his good resolutions. All the time he spent with the members of the household he devoted to the things of God, and in this way brought profit to their souls. He took great delight in the books he was read-ing, and the thought came to him to select some short but important   230 passages from the Life of Christ and the Lives of the Saints. And so he began to write very carefully in a book, as he had already begun to move a little about the house. The words of Christ he wrote in red ink and those of Our Lady in blue, on polished and lined paper in a good hand, for he was an excellent penman. Part of his time he spent in   235 writing, part in prayer. It was his greatest consolation to gaze upon the heavens and the stars, which he often did, and for long stretches at a time, because when doing so he felt within himself a power-ful urge to be serving our Lord. He gave much time to thinking about his resolve, desiring to be entirely well so that he could begin   240 his journey.

12   As he was going over in his mind what he should do on his return from Jerusalem, so as to live in perpetual penance, the thought occurred to him of joining the Carthusians[14] of Seville. He could there conceal his identity so as to be held in less esteem, and live there   245 on a strictly vegetable diet. But as the thought returned of a life of penance which he wanted to lead by going about the world, the desire of the Carthusian life grew cool, since he felt that there he would not be able to indulge the hatred he had conceived against himself. And yet, he instructed a servant of the house who was going to Burgos to   250

---

[14] A strictly contemplative religious order, combining Benedictine monachism with eremitical asceticism, founded by St. Bruno in 1084 at the Grande Chartreuse, France.

bring back information about the Carthusian Rule,[15] and the information brought to him seemed good. But for the reason given above, and because his attention was entirely occupied with the journey he was thinking of making at once, he gave up thinking about the 255 Carthusians as it was a matter that could await his return. Indeed, feeling that he was pretty well restored, he thought it was time to be up and going and told his brother so. "You know, my lord, the Duke of Nájera is aware that I have recovered. It will be good for me to go to Navarette." The Duke was there at the time. His brother led him 260 from one room to another, and with a great show of affection, begged him not to make a fool of himself. He wanted him to see what hopes the people placed in him and what influence he might have, along with other like suggestions, all with the intention of turning him from the good desire he had conceived. But, without departing from 265 the truth, for he was very scrupulous about that, he reassured him in a way that allowed him to slip away from his brother.[16]

---

[15] A monastery of the Carthusians was near Burgos and is still standing.

[16] The date of his departure from home is not certain.

17

The Spiritual Exercises

"First Principle and Foundation"
"The Two Standards"
"Comtemplation for Obtaining Love of God"

IGNATIUS OF LOYOLA (1491–1556)

INTRODUCTION

The *Spiritual Exercises* is a retreat manual, a guide-book for prayer and for prayerful decision-making based on Ignatius of Loyola's (1491–1556) own experiences of conversion and of growth in the love of God. He directed his earliest companions through these exercises; they subsequently became a fundamental basis for the religious community of priests and brothers which he founded, the Society of Jesus, popularly known as the Jesuits.

The text of the *Spiritual Exercises* is intended principally as instructions for the person who directs an individual retreatant (or a group of retreatants) in their use. Going through the full course of these exercises takes approximately one month. During that time, the retreatant withdraws from the ordinary activities of everyday life in order to concentrate on prayer—listening to and conversing with God—and the reflective evaluation of that prayer. Five exercises of prayer are normally scheduled for each day and the retreatant also meets with the director on a daily basis; during this meeting the director reviews with the retreatant what spiritual movements (consolations or desolations) have taken place in the course of that day's prayer exercises, and then proposes a focus for the exercises of the next day, based on the "points" (aspects to consider) which Ignatius provides as part of each exercise.

The pace at which a retreatant moves through the four main divisions (or "weeks") of the *Spiritual Exercises* is left to the judgment of the director. Ignatius indicates that there will be persons who are ready to make only the First Week of the Exercises, which focuses on a conversion from sin to God through a growing awareness in prayer of God's personal love and forgiveness. The first selection presented here, **"The First Principle and Foundation,"** is taken from the beginning of the *Spiritual Exercises*, where it precedes the start of the First Week. This meditation—reflecting on the fact of one's having been created—acts as a kind of introduction to the work of the exercises: to turn one from self-centeredness to God-centeredness, from illusion to truth. Because of humanity's fallen state, this realization of being created for God comes always as something of a surprise.

The Second, Third, and Fourth Weeks of the *Spiritual Exercises* focus on particular aspects of the Gospel narratives of Jesus: the Second Week on his incarnation, birth, and public ministry; the Third Week on his passion and death; and the Fourth Week on his resurrection. One principal purpose of these "weeks" is to prepare the retreatant for a God-centered decision concerning the choice of a "state of life" so that it will accord with God's plan of salvation.

At a number of key places in the course of these exercises, Ignatius proposes subject matter which is not part of the gospel narrative. The second and third selections presented here are of this kind.

The second selection, the **"Meditation on the Two Standards,"** is from the Second Week. It is placed between the exercises which focus on Jesus' incarnation and birth and those which follow the course of Jesus' public ministry. It is the first exercise with an explicit focus on the choice of a state of life. In this meditation the implicit struggle of all Christian life, set forth in an earlier reading in this course (the Gospel of Mark), is made explicit: the struggle to hear God's call in Christ against the constant temptation to make one's self the center and purpose of one's life.

The third selection, the **"Contemplation to Attain Love,"** comes at the conclusion of the Fourth Week. It returns the retreatant to a consideration of the larger context of God's plan of salvation with a focus on the active presence of God's love in all of creation and in all human activities. To the question, "Where do I find this God for whom I have been created?," the answer comes: in the whole world of created persons, things and events around you, including your own self and spirit. God is there *for you*, as a lover to a beloved. This meditation, then, immerses one in a completely sacramental view of the world.

The full text of St. Ignatius' Spiritual Exercises is available on the internet:

http://www.ccel.org/i/ignatius/exercises/exercises.html

—*Rev. Philip J. Rossi, S.J.*

TEXT[1]

Spiritual Exercises

TO CONQUER ONESELF AND REGULATE ONE'S LIFE WITHOUT DETERMINING ONESELF THROUGH ANY TENDENCY THAT IS DISORDERED

---

[1] This 1909 translation by Elder Mullan, S.J., has been slightly adjusted to be more gender inclusive, except for the First Principle and Foundation, which defied all modification short of a complete paraphrasing that would have destroyed its original simplicity and directness.

Presupposition

In order that both the one giving the Spiritual Exercises, and the one receiving them, may more help and benefit themselves, let it be presupposed that every good Christian is to be more ready to save his neighbor's proposition than to condemn it. If he cannot save it, let him inquire how the other means it; and if he means it badly, let him correct him with charity. If that is not enough, let him seek all the suitable means to bring him to mean it well, and save himself.

[The First Week]
FIRST PRINCIPLE AND FOUNDATION

Man is created to praise, reverence, and serve God our Lord, and by this means to save his soul.

And the other things on the face of the earth are created for man and that they may help him in prosecuting the end for which he is created.

From this it follows that man is to use them as much as they help him on to his end, and ought to rid himself of them so far as they hinder him as to it.

For this it is necessary to make ourselves indifferent to all created things in all that is allowed to the choice of our free will and is not prohibited to it; so that, on our part, we want not health rather than sickness, riches rather than poverty, honor rather than dishonor, long rather than short life, and so in all the rest; desiring and choosing only what is most conducive for us to the end for which we are created.

"THE TWO STANDARDS"
Preamble to Consider [Different] States [of Life]

First Preamble. The example which Christ our Lord, being under obedience to His parents, has given us for the first state,—which consists in the observance of the Commandments—having been now considered; and likewise for the second,—which is that of evangelical perfection,—when He remained in the Temple, leaving His adoptive

father and His natural Mother, to attend to the pure service of His   40
eternal Father; we will begin, at the same time contemplating His life,
to investigate and to ask in what life or state His Divine Majesty
wants to be served by us.

And so, for some introduction of it, we will, in the first Exercise
following, see the intention of Christ our Lord, and, on the contrary,   45
that of the enemy of human nature, and how we ought to dispose
ourselves in order to come to perfection in whatever state of life God
our Lord would give us to choose.

[The Second Week: The Fourth Day]

Meditation on the Two Standards

The one of Christ, our Commander-in-chief and Lord;
The other of Lucifer, mortal enemy of our human nature.

Prayer. The usual Preparatory Prayer.

First Prelude. The First Prelude is the narrative. It will be here   50
how Christ calls and wants all under His standard; and Lucifer, on the
contrary, under his.

Second Prelude. The second, a composition, seeing the place. It
will be here to see a great field of all that region of Jerusalem, where
the supreme Commander-in-chief of the good is Christ our Lord;   55
another field in the region of Babylon, where the chief of the enemy
is Lucifer.

Third Prelude. The third, to ask for what I want: and it will be
here to ask for knowledge of the deceits of the bad chief and help to
guard myself against them, and for knowledge of the true life which   60
the supreme and true Captain shows and grace to imitate Him.

First Point. The first Point is to imagine as if the chief of all the
enemy seated himself in that great field of Babylon, as in a great[2] chair
of fire and smoke, in shape horrible and terrifying.

---

[2] "great" *is inserted, perhaps in the hand of St. Ignatius.*

65   **Second Point.** The second, to consider how he issues a summons to innumerable demons and how he scatters them, some to one city and others to another, and so through all the world, not omitting any provinces, places, states, nor any persons in particular.

    Third Point. The third, to consider the discourse which he makes
70   them, and how he tells them to cast out nets, and chains; that they have first to tempt with a longing for riches—as he is accustomed to do in most cases[3] —that men may more easily come to vain honor of the world, and then to vast pride. So that the first step shall be that of riches; the second, that of honor; the third, that of pride; and from
75   these three steps he draws on to all the other vices.

    So, on the contrary, one has to imagine as to the supreme and true Captain, Who is Christ our Lord.

    First Point. The first Point is to consider how Christ our Lord puts Himself in a great field of that region of Jerusalem, in lowly
80   place, beautiful and attractive.

    Second Point. The second, to consider how the Lord of all the world chooses so many persons—Apostles, Disciples, etc.,——and sends them through all the world spreading His sacred doctrine through all states and conditions of persons.

85   **Third Point.** The third, to consider the discourse which Christ our Lord makes to all His servants and friends whom He sends on this expedition, recommending them to want to help all, by bringing them first to the highest spiritual poverty, and—if His Divine Majesty would be served and would want to choose them—no less to actual
90   poverty; the second is to be of contumely and contempt; because from these two things humility follows. So that there are to be three steps; the first, poverty against riches; the second, contumely or contempt against worldly honor; the third, humility against pride. And from these three steps let them induce to all the other virtues.

---

[3] "as he is accustomed to do in most cases" *is inserted in the Saint's handwriting.*

First Colloquy. One Colloquy to Our Lady, that she may get me   95
grace from Her Son and Lord that I may be received under His standard; and first in the highest spiritual poverty, and—if His Divine
Majesty would be served and would want to choose and receive me—
not less in actual poverty; second, in suffering contumely and injuries,
to imitate Him more in them, if only I can suffer them without the   100
sin of any person, or displeasure of His Divine Majesty; and with that
a HAIL MARY.

Second Colloquy. I will ask the same of the Son that He may get
it for me of the Father; and with that say the SOUL OF CHRIST.

Third Colloquy. I will ask the same of the Father, that He may   105
grant it to me; and say an OUR FATHER.

Note. This Exercise will be made at midnight and then a second
time in the morning, and two repetitions of this same will be made at
the hour of Mass and at the hour of Vespers, always finishing with the
three Colloquies, to Our Lady, to the Son, and to the Father; and that   110
on The Pairs which follows, at the hour before supper.

"SOUL OF CHRIST"

(Anima Christi)

Soul of Christ, sanctify me.
Body of Christ, save me.
Blood of Christ, inebriate me.
Water from the side of Christ, wash me.
Passion of Christ, strengthen me.
O good Jesus, hear me:
Within your wounds, hide me;

Suffer me not to be separated from thee;
From the malicious enemy defend me;
In the hour of death call me,
And bid me to come to thee,
That with thy saints I may praise thee,
Forever and ever. Amen

St. Ignatius glorifying God, St. Peter's Basilica, Rome

"THE CONTEMPLATION FOR OBTAINING LOVE"

Note. First, it is well to remark two things: the first is that love ought to be put more in deeds than in words.

The second, love consists in interchange between the two parties; that is to say in the lover's giving and communicating to the beloved what he has or out of what he has or can; and so, on the contrary, the beloved to the lover. So that if the one has knowledge, he give to the one who has it not. The same of honors, of riches; and so the one to the other.

Prayer. The usual Prayer.

First Prelude. The first Prelude is a composition, which is here to see how I am standing before God our Lord, and of the Angels and of the Saints interceding for me.

Second Prelude. The second, to ask for what I want. It will be here to ask for interior knowledge of so great good received, in order that being entirely grateful, I may be able in all to love and serve His Divine Majesty.

First Point. The First Point is, to bring to memory the benefits received, of Creation, Redemption and particular gifts, pondering with much feeling how much God our Lord has done for me, and how much He has given me of what He has, and then the same Lord desires to give me Himself as much as He can, according to His Divine ordination. And with this to reflect on myself, considering with much reason and justice, what I ought on my side to offer and give to His Divine Majesty, that is to say, everything that is mine, and myself with it, as one who makes an offering with much feeling:

Take, Lord, and receive all my liberty, my memory, my intellect, and all my will—all that I have and possess. Thou gavest it to me: to Thee, Lord, I return it! All is Thine, dispose of it according to all Thy will. Give me Thy love and grace, for this is enough for me.

Second Point. The second, to look how God dwells in creatures, in the elements, giving them being, in the plants vegetating, in the animals feeling in them, in men giving them to understand:[4] and so in me, giving me being, animating me, giving me sensation and making me to understand;[5] likewise making a temple of me, being created to the likeness and image of His Divine Majesty; reflecting as much on myself in the way which is said in the first Point, or in another which I feel to be better. In the same manner will be done on each Point which follows.

Third Point. The third, to consider how God works and labors for me in all things created on the face of the earth—that is, behaves like

---

[4] "giving them to understand" *is an addition, very probably in St. Ignatius' hand.*

[5] "making me to understand; likewise" *is in the Saint's handwriting, correcting a word erased, probably* "understanding".

one who labors—as in the heavens, elements, plants, fruits, cattle, etc., giving them being, preserving them, giving them vegetation and sensation, etc.

50   Then to reflect on myself.

Fourth Point. The fourth, to look how all the good things and gifts descend from above, as my poor power from the supreme and infinite power from above; and so justice, goodness, pity, mercy, etc.; as from the sun descend the rays, from the fountain the waters, etc.

Then to finish reflecting on myself, as has been said.

55   I will end with a Colloquy and an OUR FATHER.

18

"Rerum Novarum" (1891)

POPE LEO XIII (1891–1903)
(SELECTIONS)

INTRODUCTION

Leo XIII (Gioacchino Vicenzo Pecci) was born on March 2, 1810, at
Carpineto, Italy, and served as pope from February, 1878, to July, 10,
1903. Although chosen at age 68 as an interim pope, he lived to guide
the Catholic Church throughout the world for almost twenty-five
more years. During that time he led the fight against socialism, com-
munism and nihilism, and he encouraged the study of Thomism,
the objective writing of history and the use of critical methods in biblical scholarship. Most importantly, Pope Leo fostered a much needed
rapprochement between the Catholic Church and the modern world.
Not always successful in diplomatic efforts, he did manage to enhance
the stature of the papacy beyond what it had been for centuries. In his
declining years especially, he continued the centralizing of Church
power in Rome. A man of deep piety, he wrote eleven encyclicals on
the Blessed Virgin and the Rosary, and in 1900 he consecrated the
human race to the Sacred Heart of Jesus.

Leo's most enduring legacy to the Church and the world, and probably the most influential of all papal encyclicals, is his social manifesto, *Rerum Novarum* (May 15, 1891). He was the first pope to express awareness of the intolerable suffering of the urban proletariat because of the Industrial Revolution and *laissez-faire* capitalism, and to act on this by making the natural rights of the worker official church doctrine. The encyclical, justly earning Leo the title, "the workers' pope," upholds private property, the just wage, workers' rights, and trade unions. Its social teaching is based on a gospel understanding of the sacredness of the human person and the family, the moral purpose of the state, and the dignity and religious significance of work. The reader will notice how the encyclical echoes other Christian teachings that appear earlier in this volume, among them: (a) the Markan understanding of a suffering Christ based on Isaiah 53 and repeated in St. Ignatius' "Two Standards;" (b) St. Paul's 1 Corinthians 12 "body of Christ" theology, underlying Pope Leo's vision of humanity as an organic unity; and (c) the Genesis, Nicaea II and St. Ignatius ("First Principle and Foundation" and "Contemplation for Obtaining Love") teaching about the relationship human beings should have to the rest of creation.

Rerum Novarum is rightly called the "Magna Carta" of Catholic social teaching (Pius XI), but because of its nineteenth-century European view of society, the encyclical accepts uncritically a social stratification of human beings according to their differing capacity, skill, health and fortune, and gender. Consequently, although later papal writings strongly reiterate the noble social principles of *Rerum Novarum*, in adding their own insights within the changing conditions in society over this 100 year period they also attempt to avoid its limitations. In spite of its nineteenth-century characteristics, *Rerum Novarum* continues powerfully to teach basic principles of true Christian living in human community.

Through the course of the twentieth-century *Rerum Novarum* has inspired the issuance of four other social encyclicals on four of its decile anniversaries: Pope Pius XI's *Quadragesimo Anno* ("On the Fortieth Year," May 15, 1931), Pope John XXIII's *Mater et Magistra* ("Mother and Teacher," May 15, 1961), and Pope John Paul II's *Laborem Exercens* ("Engaging in Labor," September 14, 1981) and *Centesiumus Annus* ("The Centenary Year," May 1, 1991).

The attempt was made to render the translation used in this selection more gender inclusive, but in a way that would not jeopardize its original theological meaning. The complete encyclical can be found on the Internet:

http://listserv.american.edu/catholic/church/papal/leo.xiii/rerum.novarum.html

—*Rev. John D. Laurance, S.J.*

TEXT

To Our Venerable Brethren the Patriarchs, Primates, Archbishops, Bishops, and other Ordinaries of Places having Peace and Communion with the See.

1. That the spirit of revolutionary change (*Rerum novarum*), which has long been disturbing the nations of the world, should have passed   5
beyond the sphere of politics and made its influence felt in the cognate sphere of practical economics is not surprising. The elements of the conflict now raging are unmistakable, in the vast expansion of industrial pursuits and the marvelous discoveries of science; in the changed relations between employers and workers; in the enormous   10
fortunes of some few individuals, and the utter poverty of the masses; in the increased self-reliance and closer mutual combination of the working classes; as also, finally, in the prevailing moral degeneracy. The momentous gravity of the state of things now obtaining fills every mind with painful apprehension; wise people are discussing it;   15
practical people are proposing schemes; popular meetings, legislatures, and rulers of nations are all busied with it—actually there is no question which has taken a deeper hold on the public mind.

2. Therefore, venerable brethren, as on former occasions when it seemed opportune to refute false teaching, We have addressed you in   20
the interests of the Church and of the common good, and have issued

letters bearing on political power, human liberty, the Christian constitution of the State, and like matters, so have We thought it expedient now to speak on the condition of the working classes.[1] . . .

25 **3.** . . . we clearly see, and on this there is general agreement, that some opportune remedy must be found quickly for the misery and wretchedness pressing so unjustly on the majority of the working class: for the ancient workingmen's guilds were abolished in the last century, and no other protective organization took their place. Public

30 institutions and the laws set aside the ancient religion. Hence, by degrees it has come to pass that working people have been surrendered, isolated and helpless, to the hardheartedness of employers and the greed of unchecked competition. The mischief has been increased by rapacious usury, which, although more than once condemned by

35 the Church, is nevertheless, under a different guise, but with like injustice, still practiced by covetous and grasping men. To this must be added that the hiring of labor and the conduct of trade are concentrated in the hands of comparatively few; so that a small number of very rich men have been able to lay upon the teeming masses of the

40 laboring poor a yoke little better than that of slavery itself.

The Natural Right to Private Property

4. To remedy these wrongs the socialists, working on the poor man [and woman's] envy of the rich, are striving to do away with private property, and contend that individual possessions should become the common property of all, to be administered by the State or by munic-

45 ipal bodies. They hold that by thus transferring property from private individuals to the community, the present mischievous state of things will be set to rights, inasmuch as each citizen will then get his fair

---

[1] The title sometimes given to this encyclical, "On the Condition of the Working Classes," is therefore perfectly justified. A few lines after this sentence the Pope give a more comprehensive definition of the subject of *"Rerum Novarum."*

share of whatever there is to enjoy. But their contentions are so clearly powerless to end the controversy that were they carried into effect the working person himself would be among the first to suffer. They are, moreover, emphatically unjust, for they would rob the lawful possessor, distort the functions of the State, and create utter confusion in the community.

5. It is surely undeniable that, when a person engages in remunerative labor, the impelling reason and motive of his work is to obtain property, and thereafter to hold it as his very own. If one person hires out to another his strength or skill, he does so for the purpose of receiving in return what is necessary for the satisfaction of his needs; he therefore expressly intends to acquire a right full and real, not only to the remuneration, but also to the disposal of such remuneration, just as he pleases. Thus, if he lives sparingly, saves money, and, for greater security, invests his savings in land, the land, in such case, is only his wages under another form; and, consequently, a working person's little estate thus purchased should be as completely at his full disposal as are the wages he receives for his labor. But it is precisely in such power of disposal that ownership obtains, whether the property consist of land or chattels. Socialists, therefore, by endeavoring to transfer the possessions of individuals to the community at large, strike at the interests of every wage-earner, since they would deprive him of the liberty of disposing of his wages, and thereby of all hope and possibility of increasing his resources and of bettering his condition in life.

6. What is of far greater moment, however, is the fact that the remedy they propose is manifestly against justice. For, every person has by nature the right to possess property as his own. This is one of the chief points of distinction between human beings and the animal creation, for the brute has no power of self-direction, but is governed by two main instincts, which keep his powers on the alert, impel him to develop them in a fitting manner, and stimulate and determine him to action without any power of choice. One of these instincts is self-preservation, the other the propagation of the species. Both can attain their purpose by means of things which lie within range; beyond their verge the brute creation cannot go, for they are moved to action by their senses only, and in the special direction which these suggest. But

85 with a human being it is wholly different. He possesses, on the one hand, the full perfection of the animal being, and hence enjoys at least as much as the rest of the animal kind, the fruition of things material. But animal nature, however perfect, is far from representing the human being in its completeness, and is in truth but humanity's

90 humble handmaid, made to serve and to obey. It is the mind, or reason, which is the predominant element in us who are human creatures; it is this which renders a human being human, and distinguishes him essentially from the brute. And on this very account—that man alone among the animal creation is endowed with reason—it must be

95 within his right to possess things not merely for temporary and momentary use, as other living things do, but to have and to hold them in stable and permanent possession; he must have not only things that perish in the use, but those also which, though they have been reduced into use, continue for further use in after time.

100 7. This becomes still more clearly evident if human nature be considered a little more deeply. For a human being, fathoming by his faculty of reason matters without number, linking the future with the present, and being master of his own acts, guides his ways under the eternal law and the power of God, whose providence governs all

105 things. Wherefore, it is in his power to exercise his choice not only as to matters that regard his present welfare, but also about those which he deems may be for his advantage in time yet to come. Hence, man not only should possess the fruits of the earth, but also the very soil, inasmuch as from the produce of the earth he has to lay by provision

110 for the future. His needs do not die out, but forever recur; although satisfied today, they demand fresh supplies for tomorrow. Nature accordingly must have given to man a source that is stable and remaining always with him, from which he might look to draw continual supplies. And this stable condition of things he finds solely in

the earth and its fruits. There is no need to bring in the State. Man   115
precedes the State, and possesses, prior to the formation of any State,
the right of providing for the substance of his body.

8. The fact that God has given the earth for the use and enjoyment
of the whole human race can in no way be a bar to the owning of private property. For God has granted the earth to humankind in   120
general, not in the sense that all without distinction can deal with it
as they like, but rather that no part of it was assigned to any one in
particular, and that the limits of private possession have been left to
be fixed by a person's own industry, and by the laws of individual cultures. Moreover, the earth, even though apportioned among private   125
owners, ceases not thereby to minister to the needs of all, inasmuch
as there is not one who does not sustain life from what the land produces. Those who do not possess the soil contribute their labor;
hence, it may truly be said that all human subsistence is derived either
from labor on one's own land, or from some toil, some calling, which   130
is paid for either in the produce of the land itself, or in that which is
exchanged for what the land brings forth. . . .

11. With reason, then, the common opinion of humankind, little
affected by the few dissentients who have contended for the opposite
view, has found in the careful study of nature, and in the laws of   135
nature, the foundations of the division of property, and the practice
of all ages has consecrated the principle of private ownership, as being
pre-eminently in conformity with human nature, and as leading in
the most unmistakable manner to the peace and tranquillity of
human existence. The same principle is confirmed and enforced by   140
the civil laws—laws which, so long as they are just, derive from the
law of nature their binding force. The authority of the divine law adds
its sanction, forbidding us in severest terms even to covet that which
is another's: "Thou shalt not covet thy neighbor's wife; nor his house,
nor his field, nor his man-servant, nor his maid-servant, nor his ox,   145
nor his ass, nor anything that is his" (Deuteronomy 5:21).

The Sacredness of the Family

12. The rights here spoken of, belonging to each individual, are seen in much stronger light when considered in relation to one's social and domestic obligations. In choosing a state of life, it is indisputable that all are at full liberty to follow the counsel of Jesus Christ as to observing virginity, or to bind themselves by the marriage tie. No human law can abolish the natural and original right of marriage, nor in any way limit the chief and principal purpose of marriage ordained by God's authority from the beginning: "Increase and multiply" (Genesis 1:28). Hence we have the family, the "society" of one's house—a society very small, one must admit, but none the less a true society, and one older than any State. Consequently, it has rights and duties peculiar to itself which are quite independent of the State. . . .

14. The contention, then, that the civil government should at its option intrude into and exercise intimate control over the family and the household is a great and pernicious error. True, if a family finds itself in exceeding distress, utterly deprived of the counsel of friends, and without any prospect of extricating itself, it is right that extreme necessity be met by public aid, since each family is a part of the commonwealth. In like manner, if within the precincts of the household there occur grave disturbance of mutual rights, public authority should intervene to force each party to yield to the other its proper due; for this is not to deprive citizens of their rights, but justly and properly to safeguard and strengthen them. But the rulers of the commonwealth must go no further; here, nature bids them stop. . . .

The Interdependence of Capital and Labor

19. The great mistake made in regard to the matter now under consideration is to take up with the notion that class is naturally hostile to class, and that the wealthy and the working men are intended by nature to live in mutual conflict. So irrational and so false is this view that the direct contrary is the truth. Just as the symmetry of the human frame is the result of the suitable arrangement of the different

parts of the body, so in a State is it ordained by nature that these two classes should dwell in harmony and agreement, so as to maintain the balance of the body politic. Each needs the other: capital cannot do without labor, nor labor without capital. Mutual agreement results in the beauty of good order, while perpetual conflict necessarily pro-   180
duces confusion and savage barbarity. Now, in preventing such strife as this, and in uprooting it, the efficacy of Christian institutions is marvelous and manifold. First of all, there is no intermediary more powerful than religion (whereof the Church is the interpreter and guardian) in drawing the rich and the working class together, by   185
reminding each of its duties to the other, and especially of the obligations of justice.

20. Of these duties, the following bind the proletarian and the worker: fully and faithfully to perform the work which has been freely and equitably agreed upon; never to injure the property, nor to out-   190
rage the person, of an employer; never to resort to violence in defending their own cause, nor to engage in riot or disorder; and to have nothing to do with men of evil principles, who work upon the people with artful promises of great results, and excite foolish hopes which usually end in useless regrets and grievous loss. The following   195
duties bind the wealthy owner and the employer: not to look upon their work people as their bondsmen, but to respect in every man [and woman their] dignity as a person ennobled by Christian character. They are reminded that, according to natural reason and Christian philosophy, working for gain is creditable, not shameful, to   200
a person, since it enables him to earn an honorable livelihood; but to misuse people as though they were things in the pursuit of gain, or to value them solely for their physical powers—that is truly shameful and inhuman. Again justice demands that, in dealing with the working person, religion and the good of his soul must be kept in mind.   205
Hence, the employer is bound to see that the worker has time for his religious duties; that he be not exposed to corrupting influences and dangerous occasions; and that he be not led away to neglect his home and family, or to squander his earnings. Furthermore, the employer

210 must never tax his work people beyond their strength, or employ them in work unsuited to their sex and age. His great and principal duty is to give every one what is just. Doubtless, before deciding whether wages are fair, many things have to be considered; but wealthy owners and all masters of labor should be mindful of this—

220 that to exercise pressure upon the indigent and the destitute for the sake of gain, and to gather one's profit out of the need of another, is condemned by all laws, human and divine. To defraud any one of wages that are his due is a great crime which cries to the avenging anger of Heaven. "Behold, the hire of the laborers . . . which by fraud

225 has been kept back by you, crieth; and the cry of them hath entered into the ears of the Lord of Sabaoth" (James 5:4). Lastly, the rich must religiously refrain from cutting down the workers' earnings, whether by force, by fraud, or by usurious dealing; and with all the greater reason because the laboring person is, as a rule, weak and unprotected,

230 and because his slender means should in proportion to their scantiness be accounted sacred. Were these precepts carefully obeyed and followed out, would they not be sufficient of themselves to keep under all strife and all its causes?

Citizens of Heaven

21. But the Church, with Jesus Christ as her Master and Guide,

235 aims higher still. She lays down precepts yet more perfect, and tries to bind class to class in friendliness and good feeling. The things of earth cannot be understood or valued aright without taking into consideration the life to come, the life that will know no death. Exclude the idea of futurity, and forthwith the very notion of what is good and

240 right would perish; nay, the whole scheme of the universe would become a dark and unfathomable mystery. The great truth which we learn from nature herself is also the grand Christian dogma on which religion rests as on its foundation—that, when we have given up this

245 present life, then shall we really begin to live. God has not created us for the perishable and transitory things of earth, but for things heavenly and everlasting; God has given us this world as a place of exile,

and not as our abiding place. As for riches and the other things which people call good and desirable, whether we have them in abundance, or are lacking in them—so far as eternal happiness is concerned—it makes no difference; the only important thing is to use them aright. Jesus Christ, when He redeemed us with plentiful redemption, took not away the pains and sorrows which in such large proportion are woven together in the web of our mortal life. He transformed them into motives of virtue and occasions of merit; and no person can hope for eternal reward unless he follow in the blood-stained footprints of his Savior. "If we suffer with Him, we shall also reign with Him" (2 Timothy 2:12). Christ's labors and sufferings, accepted of His own free will, have marvelously sweetened all suffering and all labor. And not only by His example, but by His grace and by the hope held forth of everlasting recompense, has He made pain and grief more easy to endure; "for that which is at present momentary and light of our tribulation, worketh for us above measure exceedingly an eternal weight of glory" (2 Corinthians 4:17).

No Property Completely Private

22. Therefore, those whom fortune favors are warned that riches do not bring freedom from sorrow and are of no avail for eternal happiness, but rather are obstacles (Matthew 19:23–24); that the rich should tremble at the threatenings of Jesus Christ—threatenings so unusual in the mouth of our Lord (Luke 6:24–25)—and that a most strict account must be given to the Supreme Judge for all we possess. The chief and most excellent rule for the right use of money is one the heathen philosophers hinted at, but which the Church has traced out clearly, and has not only made known to people's minds, but has impressed upon their lives. It rests on the principle that it is one thing to have a right to the possession of money and another to have a right to use money as one ills. Private ownership, as we have seen, is the natural right of person, and to exercise that right, especially as members of society, is not only lawful, but absolutely necessary. "It is lawful," says St. Thomas Aquinas, "for a person to hold private prop-

280 erty; and it is also necessary for the carrying on of human existence."[2] But if the question be asked: How must one's possessions be used?— the Church replies without hesitation in the words of the same holy Doctor: "One should not consider his material possessions as his own, but as common to all, so as to share them without hesitation

285 when others are in need. Whence the Apostle says, 'Command the rich of this world . . . to offer with no stint, to apportion generously'."[3] True, no one is commanded to distribute to others that which is required for his own needs and those of his household; nor even to give away what is reasonably required to keep up becomingly

290 his condition in life, "for no one ought to live other than becomingly."[4] But, when what necessity demands has been supplied, and one's standing fairly taken thought for, it becomes a duty to give to the indigent out of what remains over. "From that which remains, give alms" (Luke 11:41). It is duty, not of justice (save in extreme

295 cases), but of Christian charity—a duty not enforced by human law. But the laws and judgments of human beings must yield place to the laws and judgments of Christ the true God, who in many ways urges on His followers the practice of almsgiving—"It is more blessed to give than to receive" (Acts 20:35); and who will count a kindness

300 done or refused to the poor as done or refused to Himself—"As long as you did it to one of My least brethren you did it to Me" (Matthew 25:40). To sum up, then, what has been said: Whoever has received from the divine bounty a large share of temporal blessings, whether they be external and material, or gifts of the mind, has received them

305 for the purpose of using them for the perfecting of his own nature, and, at the same time, that he may employ them, as the steward of God's providence, for the benefit of others. "He that hath a talent,"

---

[2] *Summa theologiae*, IIa–IIae, q. 61, a. 1, ad 2.

[3] Ibid.

[4] Ibid., q. 32, a. 6, Answer.

said St. Gregory the Great, "let him see that he hide it not; he that hath abundance, let him quicken himself to mercy and generosity; he that hath art and skill, let him do his best to share the use and the utility hereof with his neighbor."[5]　　　　　　　　　　　310

"Blessed are the Poor . . ."

23. As for those who possess not the gifts of fortune, they are taught by the Church that in God's sight poverty is no disgrace, and that there is nothing to be ashamed of in earning their bread by labor. This is enforced by what we see in Christ Himself, who, "whereas He was rich, for our sakes became poor" (2 Corinthians 8:9); and who, 315 being the Son of God, and God Himself, chose to seem and to be considered the son of a carpenter—nay, did not disdain to spend a great part of His life as a carpenter Himself. "Is not this the carpenter, the son of Mary?" (Mark 6:3).

24. From contemplation of this divine Model, it is more easy to 320 understand that the true worth and nobility of human beings lie in his moral qualities, that is, in virtue; that virtue is, moreover, the common inheritance of all, equally within the reach of high and low, rich and poor; and that virtue, and virtue alone, wherever found, will be followed by the rewards of everlasting happiness. Nay, God Himself 325 seems to incline rather to those who suffer misfortune; for Jesus Christ calls the poor "blessed" (Matthew 5:3); He lovingly invites those in labor and grief to come to Him for solace (Matthew 11:28); and He displays the tenderest charity toward the lowly and the oppressed. These reflections cannot fail to keep down the pride of the 330 well-to-do, and to give heart to the unfortunate; to move the former to be generous and the latter to be moderate in their desires. Thus, the separation which pride would set up tends to disappear, nor will it be difficult to make rich and poor join hands in friendly concord.

---

[5] *Hom. In Evang.*, 9, n. 7 (PL 76, 1109B)

335   **25.** But, if Christian precepts prevail, the respective classes will not
only be united in the bonds of friendship, but also in those of brotherly [and sisterly] love. For they will understand and feel that all are
children of the same common Father, who is God; that all have alike
the same last end, which is God Himself, who alone can make either
340   human beings or angels absolutely and perfectly happy; that each and
all are redeemed and made sons [and daughters] of God, by Jesus
Christ, "the first-born among many brethren"; that the blessings of
nature and the gifts of grace belong to the whole human race in common, and that from none except the unworthy is withheld the
345   inheritance of the kingdom of Heaven. "If sons, heirs also; heirs
indeed of God, and co-heirs with Christ" (Romans 8:17). Such is the
scheme of duties and of rights which is shown forth to the world by
the gospel. Would it not seem that, were society penetrated with ideas
like these, strife must quickly cease? . . .

The Church's Care of the Poor

350   **29.** The Church, moreover, intervenes directly in behalf of the
poor, by setting on foot and maintaining many associations which she
knows to be efficient for the relief of poverty. Herein, again, she has
always succeeded so well as to have even extorted the praise of her
enemies. Such was the ardor of brotherly love among the earliest
355   Christians that numbers of those who were in better circumstances
despoiled themselves of their possessions in order to relieve their
brethren; whence "neither was there any one needy among them"
(Acts 4:34). To the order of deacons, instituted in that very intent,
was committed by the Apostles the charge of the daily doles; and the
360   Apostle Paul, though burdened with the solicitude of all the churches,
hesitated not to undertake laborious journeys in order to carry the
alms of the faithful to the poorer Christians. Tertullian calls these
contributions, given voluntarily by Christians in their assemblies,
deposits of piety, because, to cite his own words, they were employed
365   "in feeding the needy, in burying them, in support of youths and

maidens destitute of means and deprived of their parents, in the care of the aged, and the relief of the shipwrecked."[6] . . .

The Obligations of the State

37. Rights must be religiously respected wherever they exist, and it is the duty of the public authority to prevent and to punish injury, and to protect every one in the possession of his or her own. Still, when there is question of defending the rights of individuals, the poor and badly off have a claim to especial consideration. The richer class have many ways of shielding themselves, and stand less in need of help from the State; whereas the mass of the poor have no resources of their own to fall back upon, and must chiefly depend upon the assistance of the State. And it is for this reason that wage-earners, since they mostly belong in the mass of the needy, should be specially cared for and protected by the government. . . .

39. When working people have recourse to a strike and become voluntarily idle, it is frequently because the hours of labor are too long, or the work too hard, or because they consider their wages insufficient. The grave inconvenience of this not uncommon occurrence should be obviated by public remedial measures; for such paralyzing of labor not only affects the masters and their work people alike, but is extremely injurious to trade and to the general interests of the public; moreover, on such occasions, violence and disorder are generally not far distant, and thus it frequently happens that the public peace is imperiled. The laws should forestall and prevent such troubles from arising; they should lend their influence and authority to the removal in good time of the causes which lead to conflicts between employers and employed.

40. The working person, too, has interests in which he should be protected by the State; and first of all, there are the interests of his soul. Life on earth, however good and desirable in itself, is not the

370

375

380

385

390

---

[6] *Apologeticus* 39 (PL 1, 533A).

395 final purpose for which human beings are created; it is only the way
and the means to that attainment of truth and that love of goodness
in which the full life of the soul consists. It is the soul which is made
after the image and likeness of God; it is in the soul that the sovereignty resides in virtue whereof human beings are commanded to rule
400 the creatures below them and to use all the earth and the ocean for
their profit and advantage. "Fill the earth and subdue it; and rule over
the fishes of the sea, and the fowls of the air, and all living creatures
that move upon the earth" (Genesis 1:28). In this respect all human
beings are equal; there is here no difference between rich and poor,
405 master and servant, ruler and ruled, "for the same is Lord over all"
(Romans 10:12). No one may with impunity outrage that human
dignity which God Himself treats with great reverence, nor stand in
the way of that higher life which is the preparation of the eternal life
of heaven. Nay, more; no one has in this matter power over himself.
410 To consent to any treatment which is calculated to defeat the end and
purpose of his being is beyond his right; he cannot give up his soul to
servitude, for it is not a human being's own rights which are here in
question, but the rights of God, the most sacred and inviolable of
rights.

415   **41**. From this follows the obligation of the cessation from work
and labor on Sundays and certain holy days. The rest from labor is
not to be understood as mere giving way to idleness; much less must
it be an occasion for spending money and for vicious indulgence, as
many would have it to be; but it should be rest from labor, hallowed
420 by religion. Rest (combined with religious observances) disposes one
to forget for a while the business of his everyday life, to turn his
thoughts to things heavenly, and to the worship which he so strictly
owes to the eternal Godhead. It is this, above all, which is the reason
and motive of Sunday rest; a rest sanctioned by God's great law of the
425 Ancient Covenant—"Remember thou keep holy the Sabbath day"
(Exodus 20:8), and taught to the world by His own mysterious "rest"
after the creation of man [in Adam and Eve]: "He rested on the seventh day from all His work which He had done" (Genesis 2:2).

Aid Societies and Worker Unions

48. In the last place, employers and workers may of themselves effect much, in the matter We are treating, by means of such associations and organizations as afford opportune aid to those who are in distress, and which draw the two classes more closely together. Among these may be enumerated societies for mutual help; various benevolent foundations established by private persons to provide for the working person, and for his widow or his orphans, in case of sudden calamity, in sickness, and in the event of death; and institutions for the welfare of boys and girls, young people, and those more advanced in years.

49. The most important of all are workers' unions, for these virtually include all the rest. History attests what excellent results were brought about by the artificers' guilds of olden times. They were the means of affording not only many advantages to the workers, but in no small degree of promoting the advancement of art, as numerous monuments remain to bear witness. Such unions should be suited to the requirements of this our age—an age of wider education, of different habits, and of far more numerous requirements in daily life. It is gratifying to know that there are actually in existence not a few associations of this nature, consisting either of workers alone, or of workers and employers together, but it were greatly to be desired that they should become more numerous and more efficient. . . .

50. The consciousness of his own weakness urges a person to call in aid from without. We read in the pages of holy Writ: "It is better that two should be together than one; for they have the advantage of their society. If one fall he shall be supported by the other. Woe to him that is alone, for when he falls he has none to lift him up" (Ecclesiastes 4:9–10). And further: "A brother that is helped by his brother is like a strong city" (Proverbs 18:19). It is this natural impulse which binds people together in civil society; and it is likewise this which leads them to join together in associations which are, it is true, lesser and not independent societies, but, nevertheless, real societies. . . .

430

435

440

445

450

455

460

64. On each of you, venerable brethren, and on your clergy and people, as an earnest of God's mercy and a mark of Our affection, we lovingly in the Lord bestow the apostolic benediction.

Given at St. Peter's in Rome, the fifteenth day of May, 1891, the fourteenth year of Our pontificate.

465

St. Peter on his teaching chair by Arnolfo di Cambio.
© Scala/Firenze

19

"Letter from a Birmingham Jail"

DR. MARTIN LUTHER KING, JR. (1929–1968)

INTRODUCTION

The movement to guarantee the civil rights of African Americans did not begin with the activism of the late 1950s.[1] Nearly a century earlier, during the Reconstruction era (1866 to 1875), Congress passed seven Civil Rights Acts to confirm the newly freed people as citizens, to safeguard their civil rights, and to ensure that they were accorded

---

[1] For a good general history, see John Hope Franklin and Alfred A. Moss, Jr., *From Slavery to Freedom: A History of African Americans* 7th ed. (New York: Alfred A. Knopf, 1994); David J. Garrow, *Protest at Selma: Martin Luther King, Jr., and the Voting Rights Act of 1965* (New Haven, CT: Yale University Press, 1978) and idem, *Bearing the Cross: Martin Luther King, Jr., and the Southern Christian Leadership Conference* (New York: William Morrow, 1986), idem, ed., *Birmingham, Alabama: 1956–1963* (Brooklyn, NY: Carlson Publishing, 1989). In addition, the University's Instructional Media Center has the PBS Documentary Series on the Civil Rights Movement, "Eyes on the Prize."

full and equal benefit of all laws.[2] The very feebleness of this legislation is insinuated by the Voting Rights Act of 1965. This is the wider historical context in which Martin Luther King's impact upon the country as well as the religious and theological, ethical and moral significance of the "Letter from a Birmingham Jail" may, perhaps, be more fully appreciated.

1. Biographical Sketch

Martin Luther King, Jr., was born January 15, 1929, in Atlanta, Georgia, into a middle-class family, the second child and first son of Alberta Christine Williams and Martin Luther King, Sr. Both his father and paternal grandfather Alfred Daniel Williams were Baptist ministers. The South in which King was born and grew to adulthood was shaped by 'Jim Crow' restrictions or segregation. This meant that African Americans were excluded by law and by custom from or segregated in parks, swimming pools, lunch counters, department stores, and theaters —simply on the basis of race.[3]

King graduated from Atlanta's Morehouse College at nineteen-years of age, then he attended Crozer Seminary in Chester, Pennsylvania. There he was exposed to Mahatma Gandhi's nonviolent activism for social change and Reinhold Niebuhr's critique of pacifism. Theologian James Cone writes that despite some "bitter

---

[2] See Albert P. Blaustein and Robert L. Zangrando, ed., *Civil Rights and the Black American: A Documentary History* (New York: Washington Square Press, 1968): On May 21, 1866, Congress passed a statute making it a criminal offense to "kidnap or carry away any other person, whether [N]egro, mulatto, or otherwise, with the intent that such person should be sold or carried into involuntary servitude, or held as a slave." Also, this statute made it a crime to "transport any [Negro] to a foreign country to be held or sold as a slave." On March 2, 1867, Congress passed "An Act to abolish and forever prohibit the System of Peonage in the Territory of New Mexico and other Parts of the United States" (227–228).

experiences" with racist whites, "the social and intellectual environ-ment at Crozer and in the surrounding area reinforced King's optimism that justice could and would be achieved with intelligent blacks and whites working together to eliminate racism."[4]

On completion of the degree from Crozer, King then enrolled in the doctoral program in systematic theology at Boston University. After completing courses and examinations, in 1953 King married Coretta Scott. The couple moved to Montgomery, Alabama, where he began duties as the full-time pastor of Dexter Avenue Baptist Church. During the first year of his pastorate, King not only distin-guished himself each Sunday in the pulpit and initiated several new ministries, but he completed his dissertation and became involved in the political life of the Montgomery community.[5]

2. The Montgomery Bus Boycott

When Rosa Parks, a seamstress at a downtown Montgomery depart-ment store, refused to surrender her bus seat to a white person on December 1, 1955, she inaugurated a new era in the black struggle for civil rights.[6] Although her arrest galvanized the community, African American leadership was "divided, contentious and appre-

---

[3] Martin Luther King, Jr., *Strive Toward Freedom* (New York: Harper, 1959), 37.

[4] Ibid., 28.

[5] The topic of King's dissertation was "A Comparison of the Conceptions of God in the Thinking of Paul Tillich and Henry Wieman."

[6] There were several 'bus incidents' in Montgomery before 1955. One of the best-known involved a fifteen-year-old high school student, Claudette Colvin, who was arrested for refusing to give up her seat to a white passen-ger. The Colvin incident did not result in a bus boycott, rather a committee of black citizens approached the manager of the bus company and the City Commission to request more courteous treatment and clarification of the seating policy.

hensive."[7] They chose King, the twenty-five-year-old newcomer, to lead the Montgomery Improvement Association.

The Montgomery boycott is legendary: For 381 days in heat and cold, in sun and rain, despite harassment by the police, intimidation by the Ku Klux Klan, jeopardized jobs, city ordinances to prohibit organized taxi transportation of the boycotters, even bombings, black people of all ages in Montgomery refused to ride buses—mostly they walked. On November 13, 1956, the U. S. Supreme Court ruled Alabama's state and local laws enforcing segregation on buses to be unconstitutional. This success made King a national, even international, figure. For the next twelve years, he devoted his life to ending racial segregation in the United States on moral and religious grounds.

3. Provocation for "Letter from a Birmingham Jail"

Despite numerous U.S. Supreme Court rulings and federal directives, racial desegregation moved forward throughout most of the South at a snail's pace, if at all. In 1963, King and the staff of the Southern Christian Leadership Conference (SCLC), working in conjunction with local black civil rights leaders and pastors, selected Birmingham, Alabama, as a test site to push the federal government to implement with speed the Supreme Court's decision. The objectives were to desegregate Birmingham's schools, public facilities, and commercial institutions, to initiate hiring and promotion of African American personnel in downtown retail stores, and to establish a biracial committee to monitor racial progress.[8]

---

[7] David Levering Lewis, "Martin Luther King, Jr., and the Promise of Nonviolent Populism," 278, in *Black Leaders of the Twentieth Century*, ed. John Hope Franklin and August Meier (Urbana: University of Illinois Press, 1982).

[8] Ibid., 285; see also, *Cone, Martin and Malcolm and America*, 120–150.

Because of mayoral elections in early March and a runoff between Albert Boutwell and Sheriff Eugene "Bull" Connor in early April, the first nonviolent demonstrations in Birmingham began on April 3, 1963.[9] Led by Sheriff Connor, the city responded with mass arrests, the use of police dogs, night sticks, tear gas, and high-pressure fire hoses. On April 12, Dr. King defied a judicial injunction to bar the protest marches and was arrested and jailed.

Eight leading white clergymen of Birmingham—Catholic, Protestant, and Jewish—in open letter denounced King as an agitator from outside the community. They condemned his conduct as unworthy of a man of God and urged the blacks of Birmingham to withdraw their support from his crusade.[10] Held in solitary confinement and deprived of adequate writing materials, King composed his response on the margins of newspapers and scraps of paper.

—*Dr. M. Shawn Copeland*

[9] Volunteers in the Birmingham campaign signed a "Commitment Card" that read in part: "1. MEDITATE daily on the teachings and life of Jesus. 2. REMEMBER always that the nonviolent movement in Birmingham seeks justice and reconciliation—not victory. 3. WALK and TALK in the manner of love, for God is love. 4. PRAY daily to be used by God in order that all men [sic] might be free. 5. SACRIFICE personal wishes in order that all men [sic] might be free. 6. OBSERVE with both friend and foe the ordinary rules of courtesy. 7. SEEK to perform regular service for others and for the world. 8. REFRAIN from the violence of fist, tongue, or heart. 9. STRIVE to be in good spiritual and bodily health. 10. FOLLOW the directions of the movement and of the captain on a demonstration," cited in John J. Ansbro, *Martin Luther King, Jr., The Making of a Mind* (1982; Maryknoll, NY: Orbis Books, 1984), vi.

[10] These men were Bishop C. C. J. Carpenter, Bishop Joseph A. Durick, Rabbi Hilton L. Grafman, Bishop Paul Hardin, Bishop Holan B. Harmon, the Reverend George M. Murray, the Reverend Edward V. Ramage, and the Reverend Earl Stallings.

TEXT

My dear Fellow Clergymen,

While confined here in the Birmingham city jail, I came across your recent statement calling our present activities "unwise and untimely." Seldom, if ever, do I pause to answer criticism of my work
5   and ideas. If I sought to answer all of the criticisms that cross my desk, my secretaries would be engaged in little else in the course of the day, and I would have no time for constructive work. But since I feel that you are men of genuine good will and your criticisms are sincerely set forth, I would like to answer your statement in what I hope
10   will be patient and reasonable terms.

I think I should give the reason for my being in Birmingham, since you have been influenced by the argument of "outsiders coming in." I have the honor of serving as president of the Southern Christian Leadership Conference, an organization operating in every southern
15   state, with headquarters in Atlanta, Georgia. We have some eighty-five affiliate organizations all across the South—one being the Alabama Christian Movement for Human Rights. Whenever necessary and possible we share staff, educational and financial resources with our affiliates. Several months ago our local affiliate here in Birm-
20   ingham invited us to be on call to engage in a nonviolent direct-action program if such were deemed necessary. We readily consented and when the hour came we lived up to our promises. So I am here, along with several members of my staff, because we were invited here. I am here because I have basic organizational ties here.

25   Beyond this, I am in Birmingham because injustice is here. Just as the eighth century prophets left their little villages and carried their "thus saith the Lord" far beyond the boundaries of their hometowns; and just as the Apostle Paul left his little village of Tarsus and carried the gospel of Jesus Christ to practically every hamlet and city of the
30   Graeco-Roman world, I too am compelled to carry the gospel of freedom beyond my particular hometown. Like Paul, I must constantly respond to the Macedonian call for aid.

Moreover, I am cognizant of the interrelatedness of all communities and states. I cannot sit idly by in Atlanta and not be concerned about what happens in Birmingham. Injustice anywhere is a threat to justice everywhere. We are caught in an inescapable network of mutuality, tied in a single garment of destiny. Whatever affects one directly affects all indirectly. Never again can we afford to live with the narrow, provincial "outside agitator" idea. Anyone who lives in the United States can never be considered an outsider anywhere in this country.

You deplore the demonstrations that are presently taking place in Birmingham. But I am sorry that your statement did not express a similar concern for the conditions that brought the demonstrations into being. I am sure that each of you would want to go beyond the superficial social analyst who looks merely at effects, and does not grapple with underlying causes. I would not hesitate to say that it is unfortunate that so called demonstrations are taking place in Birmingham at this time, but I would say in more emphatic terms that it is even more unfortunate that the white power structure of this city left the Negro community with no other alternative.

In any nonviolent campaign there are four basic steps: (1) collection of the facts to determine whether injustices are alive, (2) negotiation, (3) self-purification, and (4) direct action. We have gone through all of these steps in Birmingham. There can be no gainsaying of the fact that racial injustice engulfs this community.

Birmingham is probably the most thoroughly segregated city in the United States. Its ugly record of police brutality is known in every section of this country. Its unjust treatment of Negroes in the courts is a notorious reality. There have been more unsolved bombings of Negro homes and churches in Birmingham than any city in this nation. These are the hard, brutal and unbelievable facts. On the basis of these conditions Negro leaders sought to negotiate with the city fathers. But the political leaders consistently refused to engage in good faith negotiation.

Then came the opportunity last September to talk with some of the leaders of the economic community. In these negotiating sessions certain promises were made by the merchants—such as the promise to remove the humiliating racial signs from the stores. On the basis

70 of these promises Rev. Shuttlesworth and the leaders of the Alabama Christian Movement for Human Rights agreed to call a moratorium on any type of demonstrations. As the weeks and months unfolded we realized that we were the victims of a broken promise. The signs remained. Like so many experiences of the past we were confronted

75 with blasted hopes, and the dark shadow of a deep disappointment settled upon us. So we had no alternative except that of preparing for direct action, whereby we would present our very bodies as a means of laying our case before the conscience of the local and national community. We were not unmindful the difficulties involved. So we

80 decided to go through a process of self-purification. We started having workshops on nonviolence and repeatedly asked ourselves the questions, "Are you able to accept blows without retaliating?" "Are you able to endure the ordeals of jail?" We decided to set our direct-action program around the Easter season, realizing that with the

85 exception of Christmas, this was the largest shopping period of the year. Knowing that a strong economic withdrawal program would be the by-product of direct action, we felt that this was the best time to bring pressure on the merchants for the needed changes. Then it occurred to us that the March election was ahead and so we speedily

90 decided to postpone action until after election day. When we discovered that Mr. Connor was in the run-off, we decided again to postpone action so that the demonstrations could not be used to cloud the issues. At this time we agreed to begin our nonviolent witness the day after the run-off.

95 This reveals that we did not move irresponsibly into direct action. We too wanted to see Mr. Connor defeated; so we went through postponement after postponement to aid in this community need. After this we felt that direct action could be delayed no longer.

You may well ask, "Why direct action? Why sit-ins, marches, etc.? Isn't negotiation a better path?" You are exactly right in your call for negotiation. Indeed, this is the purpose of direct action. Nonviolent direct action seeks to create such a crisis and establish such creative tension that a community that has constantly refused to negotiate is forced to confront the issue. It seeks so to dramatize the issue that it can no longer be ignored. I just referred to the creation of tension as a part of the work of the nonviolent resister. This may sound rather shocking. But I must confess that I am not afraid of the word tension. I have earnestly worked and preached against violent tension, but there is a type of constructive nonviolent tension that is necessary for growth. Just as Socrates felt that it was necessary to create a tension in the mind so that individuals could rise from the bondage of myths and half-truths to the unfettered realm of creative analysis and objective appraisal, we must see the need of having nonviolent gadflies to create the kind of tension in society that will help men to rise from the dark depths of prejudice and racism to the majestic heights of understanding and brotherhood. So the purpose of the direct action is to create a situation so crisis packed that it will inevitably open the door to negotiation. We, therefore, concur with you in your call for negotiation. Too long has our beloved Southland been bogged down in the tragic attempt to live in monologue rather than dialogue.

One of the basic points in your statement is that our acts are untimely. Some have asked, "Why didn't you give the new administration time to act?" The only answer that I can give to this inquiry is that the new administration must be prodded about as much as the outgoing one before it acts. We will be sadly mistaken if we feel that the election of Mr. Boutwell will bring the millennium to Birmingham. While Mr. Boutwell is much more articulate and gentle than Mr. Connor, they are both segregationists, dedicated to the task of maintaining the status quo. The hope I see in Mr. Boutwell is that he will be reasonable enough to see the futility of massive resistance to desegregation. But he will not see this without pressure from the devotees of civil rights. My friends, I must say to you that we have not made a single gain in civil rights without determined legal and non-violent pressure. History is the long and tragic story of the fact that

135 privileged groups seldom give up their privileges voluntarily. Individuals may see the moral light and voluntarily give up their unjust posture; but as Reinhold Niebuhr has reminded us, groups are more immoral than individuals.

We know through painful experience that freedom is never volun-

140 tarily given by the oppressor; it must be demanded by the oppressed. Frankly, I have never yet engaged in a direct action movement that was "well-timed," according to the timetable of those who have not suffered unduly from the disease of segregation. For years now I have heard the words "Wait!" It rings in the ear of every Negro with a

145 piercing familiarity. This "Wait" has almost always meant "Never." It has been a tranquilizing thalidomide, relieving the emotional stress for a moment, only to give birth to an ill-formed infant of frustration. We must come to see with the distinguished jurist of yesterday that "justice too long delayed is justice denied." We have waited for more

150 than 340 years for our constitutional and God-given rights. The nations of Asia and Africa are moving with jetlike speed toward the goal of political independence, and we still creep at horse and buggy pace toward the gaining of a cup of coffee at a lunch counter. I guess it is easy for those who have never felt the stinging darts of segrega-

155 tion to say, "Wait." But when you have seen vicious mobs lynch your mothers and fathers at will and drown your sisters and brothers at whim; when you have seen hate-filled policemen curse, kick, brutalize and even kill your black brothers and sisters with impunity; when you see the vast majority of your twenty million Negro brothers

160 smothering in an airtight cage of poverty in the midst of an affluent society; when you suddenly find your tongue twisted and your speech stammering as you seek to explain to your six-year-old daughter why she can't go to the public amusement park that has just been advertised on television, and see tears welling up in her little eyes when she

165 is told that Funtown is closed to colored children, and see the depressing clouds of inferiority begin to form in her little mental sky, and see

her begin to distort her little personality by unconsciously developing a bitterness toward white people; when you have to concoct an answer for a five-year-old son asking in agonizing pathos: "Daddy, why do white people treat colored people so mean?"; when you take a cross-country drive and find it necessary to sleep night after night in the uncomfortable corners of your automobile because no motel will accept you; when you are humiliated day in and day out by nagging signs reading "white" and "colored"; when your first name becomes "nigger" and your middle name becomes "boy" (however old you are) and your last name becomes "John," and when your wife and mother are never given the respected title "Mrs."; when you are harried by day and haunted by night by the fact that you are a Negro, living constantly at tiptoe stance never quite knowing what to expect next, and plagued with inner fears and outer resentments; when you are forever fighting a degenerating sense of "nobodiness"; then you will understand why we find it difficult to wait. There comes a time when the cup of endurance runs over, and men are no longer willing to be plunged into an abyss of injustice where they experience the blackness of corroding despair. I hope, sirs, you can understand our legitimate and unavoidable impatience.

You express a great deal of anxiety over our willingness to break laws. This is certainly a legitimate concern. Since we so diligently urge people to obey the Supreme Court's decision of 1954 outlawing segregation in the public schools, it is rather strange and paradoxical to find us consciously breaking laws. One may well ask, "How can you advocate breaking some laws and obeying others?" The answer is found in the fact that there are two types of laws: there are just and there are unjust laws. I would agree with Saint Augustine that "An unjust law is no law at all."

Now what is the difference between the two? How does one determine when a law is just or unjust? A just law is a man-made code that squares with the moral law or the law of God. An unjust law is a code that is out of harmony with the moral law. To put it in the terms of Saint Thomas Aquinas, an unjust law is a human law that is not rooted in eternal and natural law. Any law that uplifts human personality is just. Any law that degrades human personality is unjust. All segregation statutes are unjust because segregation distorts the soul and damages the personality. It gives the segregator a false sense of superiority, and the segregated a false sense of inferiority. To use the words of Martin Buber, the greet Jewish philosopher, segregation substitutes an "I-it" relationship for the "I-thou" relationship, and ends up relegating persons to the status of things. So segregation is not only politically, economically and sociologically unsound, but it is morally wrong and sinful. Paul Tillich has said that sin is separation. Isn't segregation an existential expression of man's tragic separation, an expression of his awful estrangement, his terrible sinfulness? So I can urge men to disobey segregation ordinances because they are morally wrong.

Let us turn to a more concrete example of just and unjust laws. An unjust law is a code that a majority inflicts on a minority that is not binding on itself. This is difference made legal. On the other hand a just law is a code that a majority compels a minority to follow that it is willing to follow itself. This is sameness made legal.

Let me give another explanation. An unjust law is a code inflicted upon a minority which that minority had no part in enacting or creating because they did not have the unhampered right to vote. Who can say that the legislature of Alabama which set up the segregation laws was democratically elected? Throughout the state of Alabama all types of conniving methods are used to prevent Negroes from becoming registered voters and there are some counties without a single Negro registered to vote despite the fact that the Negro constitutes a majority of the population. Can any law set up in such a state be considered democratically structured?

These are just a few examples of unjust and just laws. There are some instances when a law is just on its face and unjust in its application. For instance, I was arrested Friday on a change of parading without a permit. Now there is nothing wrong with an ordinance which requires a permit for a parade, but when the ordinance is used

to preserve segregation and to deny citizens the First Amendment   235
privilege of peaceful assembly and peaceful protest, then it becomes
unjust.

I hope you can see the distinction I am trying to point out. In no
sense do I advocate evading or defying the law as the rabid segrega-
tionist would do. This would lead to anarchy. One who breaks an   240
unjust law must do it *openly, lovingly* (not hatefully as the white mothers did in New Orleans when they were seen on television screaming,
"nigger, nigger, nigger"), and with a willingness to accept the penalty.
I submit that an individual who breaks a law that conscience tells him
is unjust, and willingly accepts the penalty by staying in jail to arouse   245
the conscience of the community over its injustice, is in reality
expressing the very highest respect for law.

Of course, there is nothing new about this kind of civil disobedience. It was seen sublimely in the refusal of Shadrach, Meshach and
Abednego to obey the laws of Nebuchadnezzar because a higher   250
moral law was involved. It was practiced superbly by the early Christians who were willing to face hungry lions and the excruciating pain
of chopping blocks, before submitting to certain unjust laws of the
Roman Empire. To a degree academic freedom is a reality today
because Socrates practiced civil disobedience.   255

We can never forget that everything Hitler did in Germany was
"legal" and everything the Hungarian freedom fighters did in Hun-
gary was "illegal." It was "illegal" to aid and comfort a Jew in Hitler's
Germany. But I am sure that if I had lived in Germany during that
time I would have aided and comforted my Jewish brothers even   260
though it was illegal. If I lived in a Communist country today where
certain principles dear to the Christian faith are suppressed, I believe
I would openly advocate disobeying these anti-religious laws. I must
make two honest confessions to you, my Christian and Jewish brothers. First, I must confess that over the last few years I have been   265
gravely disappointed with the white moderate. I have almost reached
the regrettable conclusion that the Negro's great stumbling block in
the stride toward freedom is not the White Citizen's Counciler or the

270 Ku Klux Klanner, but the white moderate who is more devoted to "order" than to justice; who prefers a negative peace which is the absence of tension to a positive peace which is the presence of justice; who constantly says, "I agree with you in the goal you seek, but I can't agree with your methods of direct action"; who paternalistically feels that he can set the timetable for another man's freedom; who lives by

275 the myth of time and who constantly advised the Negro to wait until a "more convenient season." Shallow understanding from people of good will is more frustrating than absolute misunderstanding from people of ill will. Lukewarm acceptance is much more bewildering than outright rejection.

280 I had hoped that the white moderate would understand that law and order exist for the purpose of establishing justice, and that when they fail to do this they become dangerously structured dams that block the flow of social progress. I had hoped that the white moderate would understand that the present tension of the South is merely

285 a necessary phase of the transition from an obnoxious negative peace, where the Negro passively accepted his unjust plight, to a substance-filled positive peace, where all men will respect the dignity and worth of human personality. Actually, we who engage in nonviolent direct action are not the creators of tension. We merely bring to the surface

290 the hidden tension that is already alive. We bring it out in the open where it can be seen and dealt with. Like a boil that can never be cured as long as it is covered up but must be opened with all its pus-flowing ugliness to the natural medicines of air and light, injustice must likewise be exposed, with all of the tension its exposing creates,

300 to the light of human conscience and the air of national opinion before it can be cured.

In your statement you asserted that our actions, even though peaceful, must be condemned because they precipitate violence. But can this assertion be logically made? Isn't this like condemning the

305 robbed man because his possession of money precipitated the evil act of robbery? Isn't this like condemning Socrates because his unswerving commitment to truth and his philosophical delvings precipitated

the misguided popular mind to make him drink the hemlock? Isn't this like condemning Jesus because His unique God-consciousness and never-ceasing devotion to his will precipitated the evil act of cru- 310 cifixion? We must come to see, as federal courts have consistently affirmed, that it is immoral to urge an individual to withdraw his efforts to gain his basic constitutional rights because the quest pre- cipitates violence. Society must protect the robbed and punish the robber. 315

I had also hoped that the white moderate would reject the myth of time. I received a letter this morning from a white brother in Texas which said: "All Christians know that the colored people will receive equal rights eventually, but it is possible that you are in too great of a religious hurry. It has taken Christianity almost two thousand years to 320 accomplish what it has. The teachings of Christ take time to come to earth." All that is said here grows out of a tragic misconception of time. It is the strangely irrational notion that there is something in the very flow of time that will inevitably cure all ills. Actually time is neu- tral. It can be used either destructively or constructively. I am coming 325 to feel that the people of ill will have used time much more effectively than the people of good will. We will have to repent in this genera- tion not merely for the vitriolic words and actions of the bad people, but for the appalling silence of the good people. We must come to see that human progress never rolls in on wheels of inevitability. It comes 330 through the tireless efforts and persistent work of men willing to be co-workers with God, and without this hard word time itself becomes an ally of the forces of social stagnation. We must use time creatively, and forever realize that the time is always ripe to do right. Now is the time to make real the promise of democracy, and transform our pend- 335 ing national elegy into a creative psalm of brotherhood. Now is the time to lift our national policy from the quicksand of racial injustice to the solid rock of human dignity.

You spoke of our activity in Birmingham as extreme. At first I was rather disappointed that fellow clergymen would see my nonviolent 340 efforts as those of the extremist. I started thinking about the fact that

I stand in the middle of two opposing forces in the Negro community. One is a force of complacency made up of Negroes who, as a result of long years of oppression, have been so completely drained of self-respect and a sense of "somebodiness" that they have adjusted to segregation, and, of a few Negroes in the middle class who, because of a degree of academic and economic security, and because at points they profit by segregation, have unconsciously become insensitive to the problems of the masses. The other force is one of bitterness and hatred, and comes perilously close to advocating violence. It is expressed in the various black nationalist groups that are springing up over the nation, the largest and best known being Elijah Muhammad's Muslim movement. This movement is nourished by the contemporary frustration over the continued existence of racial discrimination. It is made up of people who have lost faith in America, who have absolutely repudiated Christianity, and who have concluded that the white man is an incurable "devil." I have tried to stand between these two forces, saying that we need not follow the "do-nothingism" of the complacent or the hatred and despair of the black nationalist. There is the more excellent way of love and nonviolent protest. I'm grateful to God that, through the Negro church, the dimension of nonviolence entered our struggle. If this philosophy had not emerged, I am convinced that by now many streets of the South would be flowing with floods of blood. And I am further convinced that if our white brothers dismiss us as "rabble-rousers" and "outside agitators" those of us who are working through the channels of nonviolent direct action and refuse to support our nonviolent efforts, millions of Negroes, out of frustration and despair, will seek solace and security in black nationalist ideologies, a development that will lead inevitably to a frightening racial nightmare.

Oppressed people cannot remain oppressed forever. The urge for freedom will eventually come. This is what happened to the American Negro. Something within has reminded him of his birthright of freedom; something without has reminded him that he can gain it. Consciously and unconsciously, he has been swept in by what the Germans call the *Zeitgeist*, and with his black brothers of Africa, and his brown and yellow brothers of Asia, South America and the Caribbean, he is moving with a sense of cosmic urgency toward the promised land of racial justice. Recognizing this vital urge that has engulfed the Negro community, one should readily understand public demonstrations. The Negro has many pent-up resentments and latent frustrations. He has to get them out. So let him march sometime; let him have his prayer pilgrimages to the city hall; understand why he must have sit-ins and freedom rides. If his repressed emotions do not come out in these nonviolent ways, they will come out in ominous expressions of violence. This is not a threat; it is a fact of history. So I have not said to my people "get rid of your discontent." But I have tried to say that this normal and healthy discontent can be channelized through the creative outlet of nonviolent direct action. Now this approach is being dismissed as extremist. I must admit that I was initially disappointed in being so categorized.

But as I continued to think about the matter I gradually gained a bit of satisfaction from being considered an extremist. Was not Jesus an extremist in love—"Love your enemies, bless them that curse you, pray for them that despitefully use you." Was not Amos an extremist for justice—"Let justice roll down like waters and righteousness like a mighty stream." Was not Paul an extremist for the gospel of Jesus Christ—"I bear in my body the marks of the Lord Jesus." Was not Martin Luther an extremist—"Here I stand; I can do none other so help me God." Was not John Bunyan an extremist—"I will stay in jail to the end of my days before I make a butchery of my conscience." Was not Abraham Lincoln an extremist—"This nation cannot survive half slave and half free." Was not Thomas Jefferson an extremist—"We hold these truths to be self-evident, that all men are created equal." So the question is not whether we will be extremist but what kind of extremist will we be. Will we be extremists for hate or will we be extremists for love? Will we be extremists for the preservation of injustice—or will we be extremists for the cause of justice? In that dramatic scene on Calvary's hill, three men were crucified. We must not forget that all three were crucified for the same crime—the crime of extremism. Two were extremists for immorality, and thusly fell below their environment. The other, Jesus Christ, was an extremist for love, truth and goodness, and thereby rose above his environment. So, after all, maybe the South, the nation and the world are in dire need of creative extremists.

I had hoped that the white moderate would see this. Maybe I was too optimistic. Maybe I expected too much. I guess I should have realized that few members of a race that has oppressed another race can understand or appreciate the deep groans and passionate yearnings of those that have been oppressed and still fewer have the vision to see that injustice must be rooted out by strong, persistent and determined action. I am thankful, however, that some of our white brothers have grasped the meaning of this social revolution and committed themselves to it. They are still all too small in quantity, but they are big in quality. Some like Ralph McGill, Lillian Smith, Harry Golden and James Dabbs have written about our struggle in eloquent, prophetic and understanding terms. Others have marched with us down nameless streets of the South. They have languished in filthy roach-infested jails, suffering the abuse and brutality of angry policemen who see them as "dirty nigger-lovers." They, unlike so many of their moderate brothers and sisters, have recognized the urgency of the moment and sensed the need for powerful "action" antidotes to combat the disease of segregation.

Let me rush on to mention my other disappointment. I have been so greatly disappointed with the white church and its leadership. Of course, there are some notable exceptions. I am not unmindful of the fact that each of you has taken some significant stands on this issue. I commend you, Rev. Stallings, for your Christian stance on this past Sunday, in welcoming Negroes to your worship service on a non-segregated basis. I commend the Catholic leaders of this state for integrating Spring Hill College[11] several years ago.

---

[11] A Jesuit liberal arts college in Mobile, Alabama.

But despite these notable exceptions I must honestly reiterate that I have been disappointed with the church. I do not say that as one of the negative critics who can always find something wrong with the church. I say it as a minister of the gospel, who loves the church; who was nurtured in its bosom; who has been sustained by its spiritual blessings and who will remain true to it as long as the cord of life shall lengthen.

I had the strange feeling when I was suddenly catapulted into the leadership of the bus protest in Montgomery several years ago that we would have the support of the white church. I felt that the white ministers, priests and rabbis of the South would be some of our strongest allies. Instead, some have been outright opponents, refusing to understand the freedom movement and misrepresenting its leaders; all too many others have been more cautious than courageous and have remained silent behind the anesthetizing security of the stained-glass windows.

In spite of my shattered dreams of the past, I came to Birmingham with the hope that the white religious leadership of this community would see the justice of our cause, and with deep moral concern, serve as the channel through which our just grievances would get to the power structure. I had hoped that each of you would understand. But again I have been disappointed. I have heard numerous religious leaders of the South call upon their worshippers to comply with a desegregation decision because it is the *law,* but I have longed to hear white ministers say, "Follow this decree because integration is morally *right* and the Negro is your brother." In the midst of blatant injustices inflicted upon the Negro, I have watched white churches stand on the sideline and merely mouth pious irrelevancies and sanctimonious trivialities. In the midst of a mighty struggle to rid our nation of racial and economic injustice, I have heard so many ministers say, "Those are social issues with which the gospel has no real concern," and I have watched so many churches commit themselves to a completely otherworldly religion which made a strange distinction between body and soul, the sacred and the secular.

445

450

455

460

465

470

475

So here we are moving toward the exit of the twentieth century with a religious community largely adjusted to the status quo, standing as a taillight behind other community agencies rather than a headlight leading men to higher levels of justice.

480   I have traveled the length and breadth of Alabama, Mississippi and all the other southern states. On sweltering summer days and crisp autumn mornings I have looked at her beautiful churches with their lofty spires pointing heavenward. I have beheld the impressive outlay of her massive religious education buildings. Over and over again I

485 have found myself asking: "What kind of people worship here? Who is their God? Where were their voices when the lips of Governor Barnett dripped with words of interposition and nullification? Where were they when Governor Wallace gave the clarion call for defiance and hatred? Where were their voices of support when tired, bruised

490 and weary Negro men and women decided to rise from the dark dungeons of complacency to the bright hills of creative protest?"

Yes, these questions are still in my mind. In deep disappointment, I have wept over the laxity of the church. But be assured that my tears have been tears of love. There can be no deep disappointment where

495 there is not deep love. Yes, I love the church; I love her sacred walls. How could I do otherwise? I am in the rather unique position of being the son, the grandson and the great-grandson of preachers. Yes, I see the church as the body of Christ. But, oh! How we have blemished and scarred that body through social neglect and fear of being

500 nonconformists.

There was a time when the church was very powerful. It was during that period when the early Christians rejoiced when they were deemed worthy to suffer for what they believed. In those days the church was not merely a thermometer that recorded the ideas and

505 principles of popular opinion; it was a thermostat that transformed the mores of society. Wherever the early Christians entered a town the power structure got disturbed and immediately sought to convict them for being "disturbers of the peace" and "outside agitators." But they went on with the conviction that they were "a colony of heaven,"

and had to obey God rather than man. They were small in number   510
but big in commitment. They were too God-intoxicated to be "astro-
nomically intimidated." They brought an end to such ancient evils as
infanticide and gladiatorial contest.

Things are different now. The contemporary church is often a
weak, ineffectual voice with an uncertain sound. It is so often the   515
arch-supporter of the status quo. Far from being disturbed by the
presence of the church, the power structure of the average community is consoled by the church's silent and often vocal sanction of
things as they are.

But the judgment of God is upon the church as never before. If the   520
church of today does not recapture the sacrificial spirit of the early
church, it will lose its authentic ring, forfeit the loyalty of millions,
and be dismissed as an irrelevant social club with no meaning for the
twentieth century. I am meeting young people every day whose disappointment with the church has risen to outright disgust.   525

Maybe again, I have been too optimistic. Is organized religion too
inextricably bound to the status quo to save our nation and the
world? Maybe I must turn my faith to the inner spiritual church, the
church within the church, as the true *ecclesia* and the hope of the
world. But again I am thankful to God that some noble souls from   530
the ranks of organized religion have broken loose from the paralyzing
chains of conformity and joined us as active partners in the struggle
for freedom. They have left their secure congregations and walked the
streets of Albany, Georgia, with us. They have gone through the
highways of the South on tortuous rides for freedom. Yes, they have   535
gone to jail with us. Some have been kicked out of their churches, and
lost support of their bishops and fellow ministers. But they have gone
with the faith that right defeated is stronger than evil triumphant.
These men have been the leaven in the lump of the race. Their witness has been the spiritual salt that has preserved the true meaning of   540
the gospel in these troubled times. They have carved a tunnel of hope
through the dark mountain of disappointment.

I hope the church as a whole will meet the challenge of this decisive hour. But even if the church does not come to the aid of justice,
545 I have no despair about the future. I have no fear about the outcome
of our struggle in Birmingham, even if our motives are presently mis-
understood. We will reach the goal of freedom in Birmingham and all
over the nation, because the goal of America is freedom. Abused and
scorned though we may be, our destiny is tied up with the destiny of
550 America. Before the Pilgrims landed at Plymouth we were here.
Before the pen of Jefferson etched across the pages of history the
majestic words of the Declaration of Independence, we were here. For
more than two centuries our foreparents labored in this country without wages; they made cotton king; and they built the homes of their
555 masters in the midst of brutal injustice and shameful humiliation—
and yet out of a bottomless vitality they continued to thrive and
develop. If the inexpressible cruelties of slavery could not stop us, the
opposition we now face will surely fail. We will win our freedom
because the sacred heritage of our nation and the eternal will of God
560 are embodied in our echoing demands.

I must close now. But before closing I am impelled to mention one
other point in your statement that troubled me profoundly. You
warmly commended the Birmingham police force for keeping "order"
and "preventing violence." I don't believe you would have so warmly
565 commended the police force if you had seen its angry violent dogs literally biting six unarmed, nonviolent Negroes. I don't believe you
would so quickly commend the policemen if you would observe their
ugly and inhuman treatment of Negroes here in the city jail; if you
would watch them push and curse old Negro women and young
570 Negro girls; if you would see them slap and kick old Negro men and
young boys; if you will observe them, as they did on two occasions,
refuse to give us food because we wanted to sing our grace together.
I'm sorry that I can't join you in your praise for the police department.

575 It is true that they have been rather disciplined in their public han-
dling of the demonstrators. In this sense they have been rather

publicly "nonviolent." But for what purpose? To preserve the evil system of segregation. Over the last few years I have consistently
preached that nonviolence demands that the means we use must be
as pure as the ends we seek. So I have tried to make it clear that it is   580
wrong to use immoral means to attain moral ends. But now I must
affirm that it is just as wrong, or even more so, to use moral means to
preserve immoral ends. Maybe Mr. Connor and his policemen have
been rather publicly nonviolent, as Chief Pritchett was in Albany,
Georgia, but they have used the moral means of nonviolence to main-   585
tain the immoral end of flagrant racial injustice. T.S. Eliot has said
that there is no greater treason than to do the right deed for the wrong
reason.

I wish you had commended the Negro sit-inners and demonstrators of Birmingham for their sublime courage, their willingness to   590
suffer and their amazing discipline in the midst of the most inhuman
provocation. One day the South will recognize its real heroes. They
will be the James Merediths, courageously and with a majestic sense
of purpose facing jeering and hostile mobs and the agonizing loneli-
ness that characterizes the life of the pioneer. They will be old,   595
oppressed, battered Negro women, symbolized in a seventy-two-year-
old woman of Montgomery, Alabama, who rose up with a sense of
dignity and with her people decided not to ride the segregated buses,
and responded to one who inquired about her tiredness with ungram-
matical profundity: "My feet is tired, but my soul is rested." They will   600
be the young high school and college students, young ministers of the
gospel and a host of their elders courageously and nonviolently sit-
ting-in at lunch counters and willingly going to jail for conscience's
sake. One day the South will know that when these disinherited children of God sat down at lunch counters they were in reality standing   605
up for the best in the American dream and the most sacred values in
our Judeo-Christian heritage, and thusly, carrying our whole nation
back to those great wells of democracy which were dug deep by the
Founding Fathers in the formulation of the Constitution and the
Declaration of Independence.   610

Never before have I written a letter this long (or should I say a book?). I'm afraid that it is much too long to take your precious time. I can assure you that it would have been much shorter if I had been writing from a comfortable desk, but what else is there to do when you are alone for days in the dull monotony of a narrow jail cell other than write long letters, think strange thoughts, and pray long prayers?

If I have said anything in this letter that is an overstatement of the truth and is indicative of an unreasonable impatience, I beg you to forgive me. If I have said anything in this letter that is an understatement of the truth and is indicative of my having a patience that makes me patient with anything less than brotherhood, I beg God to forgive me.

I hope this letter finds you strong in the faith. I also hope that circumstances will soon make it possible for me to meet each of you, not as an integrationist or a civil rights leader, but as a fellow clergyman and a Christian brother. Let us all hope that the dark clouds of racial prejudice will soon pass away and the deep fog of misunderstanding will be lifted from our fear-drenched communities and in some not too distant tomorrow the radiant stars of love and brotherhood will shine over our great nation with all or their scintillating beauty.

Yours for the cause of Peace and Brotherhood,

—Martin Luther King, Jr.[12]

---

[12] Martin Luther King, Jr., *Why We Can't Wait* (New York: Harper & Row, 1963, 1964). The American Friends Committee first published this essay as a pamphlet. It has probably been reprinted more than anything else Dr. King wrote.

20

"Sacrosanctum Concilium," 1–14 (1963)

THE SECOND VATICAN COUNCIL (1962–1965)

INTRODUCTION

What Is an "Ecumenical Council?"

Councils within the Catholic Church take place on various levels of Church life. (1) "Diocesan councils," also called "synods," are convocations by the local bishop of representative clergy and laity in order to deal with matters of diocesan church discipline. (2) "Provincial councils" are meetings of the metropolitan archbishop with his suffragan bishops. (3) Assemblies of all the bishops of a given nation are called "plenary councils." Note that the so-called "Synod of Bishops" is a standing committee of bishops from around the world, some elected, some chosen, convened occasionally by the pope to work with him in guiding the universal church.

Finally, (4) "ecumenical councils," also called "general councils," are gatherings of all the bishops of the world (Greek: *oikumene*=

housed, i.e., inhabited, world) in union with the bishop of Rome, the pope, who acts as presider and final arbiter of their decrees and decisions. Ecumenical councils are named for their location. The latest ecumenical council was the second to take place in St. Peter's Basilica in the Vatican City. Hence its name: "Vatican II." If one considers Nicaea I in A.D. 325 the first ecumenical council, then Vatican II is the twenty-first.

Why Do Ecumenical Councils Take Place, and Why in Particular a Vatican II?

Previous ecumenical councils were all summoned, either by emperor or pope, whenever the church was faced with a crisis, arising most often from doctrines considered erroneous that threatened Church unity in the integrity of the faith received from the apostles. In his announcement of January 25, 1959, Pope John XXIII called for a council with a different set of purposes. Instead of being a "doctrinal council," clarifying articles of faith against distorted teachings, it would be a "pastoral council," concerned with renewing the ongoing life of the Church. His aims, enunciated later in the very first paragraph of the first document of the council, "The Constitution on the Sacred Liturgy," were three-fold:

(1) help foster an **inner spiritual renewal** of the Church;

(2) set in motion a **modernization** of its forms and institutions ("*aggiornamento*");

(3) lead through **ecumenism** to greater unity among all Christians.

Pope John XXIII (Guiseppe Roncalli) opened the council on October 11, 1962. About 2,400 bishops participated, many with theological advisers ("*periti*"), along with Catholic and non-Catholic observers. When Pope John died in 1963, Pope Paul VI (Giovanni Battista Montini) continued the council and its aims through its remaining deliberations and the enactments of all of its conciliar decrees, presiding at its closing on December 8, 1965.

What Teaching Authority Do Ecumenical Councils Have?

The pope and bishops as the "magisterium" (Latin: teaching office) are the Spirit-guaranteed[1] articulators of the faith possessed by the whole Church, so that "reception," rightly understood,[2] by the faithful is an essential element in their teaching function. An ecumenical council, then, where bishops from all over the world gather in formal session, is the highest teaching authority in the Catholic Church. Consequently, conciliar documents have a faith-claim on the members of the Church far surpassing even that of papal encyclicals. At the same time, all pronouncements of the "*extraordinary* magisterium"— declarations whether by the pope alone or with an ecumenical council that a particular doctrine is infallibly true—necessarily demand full faith consent by Catholics, and so possess equal authority. As a pastoral council, however, Vatican II did not make any such declarations and so its teachings remain on the level of what is called the "*ordinary* magisterium," the authoritative explanations of existing faith doctrines by the pope and bishops in the ongoing life of the Church. Nevertheless, as expressing an almost unanimous agreement in the faith of the whole episcopal college, the documents of Vatican II when taken together do possess, in their indicating a single new direction for the Church, a near infallible authority for the Catholic Church. One can hardly deny the whole thrust and spirit of Vatican II and still be considered a Catholic.

On What Topics Did Vatican II Teach?

The council issued **16** official documents:

2 "dogmatic constitutions": On the Church ("*Lumen Gentium*") and On Divine Revelations ("*Dei Verbum*");

---

1 See Matthew 16:16–19; 28:20; John 14:16–17; Acts 2:1–4; 1 Timothy 4:11–14.

2 See Avery Dulles, S.J., "*Sensus Fidelium,*" in: *America*, 1 Nov 1986, pp. 240–243, 263–264.

1 **"constitution":** On the Sacred Liturgy ("*Sacrosanctum Concilium*");

1 **"pastoral constitution":** The Church in the Modern World ("*Gaudium et Spes*");

9 **"decrees":** On the Instruments of Social Communication ("*Inter Mirifica*"), On Ecumenism ("*Unitatis Redintegratio*"), On Eastern Catholic Churches ("*Orientalium Ecclesiarum*"), On the Bishops' Pastoral Office in the Church ("*Christus Dominus*"), On Priestly Formation ("*Optatum Totius*"), On the Appropriate Renewal of Religious Life ("*Perfectae Caritatis*"), On the Laity ("*Apostolicam Actuositatem*"), On the Ministry and Life of Priests ("*Presbyterorum Ordinis*"), and On the Missions ("*Ad Gentes*"); and:

3 **"declarations":** On Christian Education ("*Gravissiumum Educationis*"), On the Relationship of the Church to Non-Christian Religions ("*Nostra Aetate*"), and On Religious Freedom ("*Dignitatis Humanae*").

What Did the Council Teach in Regard to the Church's Liturgy?

The first of the council's decrees derives its name, as do all Church documents, from its opening words in the original Latin, "*Sacrosanctum Concilium*" ("This most holy council . . ."). Promulgated on **December 4, 1963,** this "Constitution on the Sacred Liturgy" presents the Catholic Church's faith-understanding of the nature and role of the liturgy in Christian life, and sets down principles and norms for the renewal of the liturgy to foster that life. The major teachings of this "Constitution on the Sacred Liturgy" include the following:

1. ***Summit and Source of Church Life:*** The Church both acts as and becomes Christ's sacrament in the world through (a) **witness** and (b) **service** to others, but most explicitly and decidedly through (c) the traditional forms of her **sacred liturgy** (par. 9–10).

2. ***The Paschal Mystery.*** As the fullness of God's self-communication in human history, Jesus Christ is present and active in his **saving events**—his passion, death and resurrection—in the Church's liturgy (par. 5, 7).

3. ***Participation in the Faith of Christ.*** In the liturgy Christ saves and sanctifies the Church in and through the Church's own symbolic **self-offering in faith** (par. 6–8).

4. ***Active Participation.*** Thus, by its very nature authentic Christian liturgy as expression of faith demands the full, conscious, and active participation of **all the members** of the Church (par. 11, 14).

5. ***Liturgy Reformable.*** Traditional liturgical forms witness both to Christ in his saving events and to the Church's faith in Christ through the ages as "the same, yesterday, today and forever" (Hebrews 13:8). But the Church can and should modify the liturgy whenever necessary to insure, within **changing cultures**, the communication of the Church's **unchanging faith** (par. 4).

The full texts of all the Vatican II documents are available on the Internet: http://alapadre.net/vatican2.html

—*Rev. John D. Laurance, S.J.*

TEXT[3]

PAUL, BISHOP
SERVANT OF THE SERVANTS OF GOD
TOGETHER WITH THE FATHERS OF THE SACRED
COUNCIL FOR EVERLASTING MEMORY

1. It is the goal of this most sacred Council to intensify the daily growth of Catholics in Christian living; to make more responsive to the requirements of our times those Church observances which are

5

---

[3] The original translation has been changed slightly to make the text more gender inclusive.—Ed., *Introduction to Theology.*

open to adaptation; to nurture whatever can contribute to the unity of all who believe in Christ; and to strengthen those aspects of the Church which can help summon all of mankind into her embrace. Hence the Council has special reasons for judging it a duty to provide for the renewal and fostering of the liturgy.

2. For it is through the liturgy, especially the divine Eucharistic Sacrifice, that "the work of our redemption is exercised."[4] The liturgy is thus the outstanding means by which the faithful can express in their lives, and manifest to others, the mystery of Christ and the real nature of the true Church.[5] It is of the essence of the Church that she be both human and divine, visible and yet invisibly endowed, eager to act and yet devoted to contemplation, present in this world and yet not at home in it. She is all these things in such a way that in her the human is directed and subordinated to the divine, the visible likewise to the invisible, action to contemplation, and this present world to that city yet to come, which we seek (cf. Heb.13:14). Day by day the liturgy builds up those within the Church into the Lord's holy temple, into a spiritual dwelling for God (cf. Eph. 2:21–22)—an enterprise which will continue until Christ's full stature is achieved (cf. Eph. 4:13). At the same time the liturgy marvelously fortifies the faithful in their capacity to preach Christ. To outsiders the liturgy thereby reveals the Church as a sign raised above the nations (cf. Is. 11:12). Under this sign the scattered sons and daughters of God are being gathered into one (cf. Jn. 11:52) until there is one fold and one shepherd (cf. Jn. 10:16).

3. Therefore this most sacred Council judges that the following principles concerning the promotion and reform of the liturgy should be called to mind, and that practical norms should be established.

---

[4] *Secret* (prayer in the Mass now called Prayer over the Offerings) for the ninth Sunday after Pentecost.

[5] Liturgy is seen as something profound rather than merely external. In many ways this Constitution is the germ of the Constitution on the Church, promulgated on Nov. 21, 1964.

Outside View of St. Peter's Basilica, Rome.
Photo by John D. Laurance, S.J.

Among these principles and norms there are some which can and should be applied both to the Roman rite and also to all the other rites. The practical norms which follow, however, should be taken as pertaining only to the Roman rite, except for those which, in the very 40 nature of things, affect other rites as well.[6]

4. Finally, in faithful obedience to tradition, this most sacred Council declares that holy Mother Church holds all lawfully acknowledged rites to be of equal authority and dignity; that she wishes to preserve them in the future and to foster them in every way. 50 The Council also desires that, where necessary, the rites be carefully and thoroughly revised in the light of sound tradition, and that they be given new vigor to meet the circumstances and needs of modern times.

CHAPTER I

55 ## GENERAL PRINCIPLES FOR THE RESTORATION AND PROMOTION OF THE SACRED LITURGY

I. The Nature of the Sacred Liturgy and Its Importance in the Church's Life

60 **5.** God, who "wishes all people to be saved and come to the knowledge of the truth" (1 Tim. 2:4), "in many and various ways. . . spoke of old to our fathers by the prophets"[7] (Heb. 1:1). When the fullness of time had come He sent His Son, the Word made flesh, anointed by the Holy Spirit, to preach the gospel to the poor, to heal the con- 65 trite of heart (cf. Is. 61:1; Lk. 4:18), to be a "bodily and spiritual

---

[6] The rites of the Eastern Church, which are in no way inferior to the Roman rite, are envisioned here only in the broadest principles, for details, they follow their own venerable traditions.

[7] Revised Standard Version (Confraternity: "at sundry times and in divers manners")—Ed.

medicine,"[8] the Mediator between God and man (cf. 1 Tim. 2:5).[9]
For His humanity, united with the person of the Word, was the
instrument of our salvation. Thus in Christ "there came forth the perfect satisfaction needed for our reconciliation, and we received the
means for giving worthy worship to God."[10]

70

The wonders wrought by God among the people of the Old Testament were but a prelude to the work of Christ the Lord in
redeeming mankind and giving perfect glory to God. He achieved
His task principally by the paschal mystery of His blessed passion,
resurrection from the dead, and glorious ascension, whereby "dying,
he destroyed our death and, rising, he restored our life."[11] For it was
from the side of Christ as He slept the sleep of death upon the cross
that there came forth the wondrous sacrament which is the whole
Church.[12]

75

6. Just as Christ was sent by the Father, so also He sent the apostles, filled with the Holy Spirit. This He did so that, by preaching the
gospel to every creature (cf. Mk. 16:15), they might proclaim that the
Son of God, by His death and resurrection, had freed us from the
power of Satan (cf. Acts 26: 18) and from death, and brought us into
the kingdom of His Father. His purpose was also that they might
exercise the work of salvation which they were proclaiming, by means
of sacrifice and sacraments, around which the entire liturgical life

80

85

---

[8] St. Ignatius of Antioch, "To the Ephesians," 7, 2; ed. F. X. Funk, Patres Apostolici I, Tübingen, 1901, p. 218.

[9] The central position of Christ as our Mediator is the theme of Pius XII's important encyclical, Mediator Dei, which was the Magna Carta of the litur-gical renewal (1947). The present Constitution, however, goes far beyond its development.

[10] Sacramentarium Veronense (Leonianum); ed. C. Mohlberg, Rome, 1956 n. 1265.

[11] Easter Preface in the Roman Missal.

[12] Cf. St. Augustine, "Enarr. in Ps. 138" 2, Corpus Chritianorum XL, Tournai, 1956, p. 1991, and prayer after the second lesson for Holy Saturday, as it was in the Roman Missal before the restoration of Holy Week.

revolves. Thus, by baptism, human beings are plunged into the
paschal mystery of Christ: they die with Him, are buried with Him,
90   and rise with Him (cf. Rom. 6:4; Eph. 2:6; Col. 3:1; 2 Tim. 2:11);
they receive the spirit of adoption as sons "by virtue of which we cry:
Abba, Father" (Rom. 8:15), and thus become those true adorers
whom the Father seeks (cf. Jn. 4:23). In like manner, as often as they
eat the supper of the Lord they proclaim the death of the Lord until
95   He comes (cf. 1 Cor. 11:26). For that reason, on the very day of Pentecost, when the Church appeared before the world, "those who
received the word" of Peter "were baptized." And "they continued
steadfastly in the teaching of the apostles and in the communion of
the breaking of the bread and in the prayers . . . praising God and
100 being in favor with all the people" (Acts 2:41–47). From that time
onward the Church has never failed to come together to celebrate the
paschal mystery: reading "in all the Scriptures the things referring to
himself" (Lk. 24:27), celebrating the Eucharist in which "the victory
and triumph of his death are again made present,[13] and at the same
105 time giving thanks "to God for his unspeakable gift" (2 Cor. 9:15) in
Christ Jesus, "to the praise of his glory" (Eph. 1:12), through the
power of the Holy Spirit.

7. To accomplish so great a work, Christ is always present in His
Church, especially in her liturgical celebrations. He is present in the
110 sacrifice of the Mass, not only in the person of His minister, "the same
one now offering, through the ministry of priests, who formerly
offered himself on the cross,"[14] but especially under the Eucharistic
species. By His power He is present in the sacraments, so that when
a person baptizes it is really Christ Himself who baptizes.[15] He is pre-

---

[13] *Council of Trent, Session 13, Oct. 11, 1551, Decree on the Holy Eucharist c. 5:
Concilium Tridentinum, Diariorum, Actorum, Epistolarum, Tractatuum nova
collectio, ed. Soc. Goerresiana, VII, Actorum pars IV, Freiburg im Breisgau,
1961, p. 202.*

[14] *Council of Trent, Session 22, Sept. 17, 1562, Doctrine on the Holy Sacrifice of
the Mass, c. 2: Concilium Tridentinum, ed. cit., VIII, Actorum pars V, Freiburg
im Breisgau, 1919, p. 960.*

[15] *Cf. St. Augustine, "In Ioannis Evangelium tractatus VI," c. 1, n. 7; PL 35, 1428.*

sent in His word, since it is He Himself who speaks when the holy   115
Scriptures are read in the church. He is present, finally, when the
Church prays and sings, for He promised: "Where two or three are
gathered together for my sake, there am I in the midst of them" (Mt.
18:20).

Christ indeed always associates the Church with Himself in the   120
truly great work of giving perfect praise to God and making men
holy. The Church is His dearly beloved Bride who calls to her Lord,
and through Him offers worship to the Eternal Father.

Rightly, then, the liturgy is considered as an exercise of the priestly
office of Jesus Christ. In the liturgy the sanctification of people is   125
manifested by signs perceptible to the senses, and is effected in a way
which is proper to each of these signs; in the liturgy full public worship is performed by the Mystical Body of Jesus Christ, that is, by the
Head and His members.[16]

From this it follows that every liturgical celebration, because it is   130
an action of Christ the priest and of His Body the Church, is a sacred
action surpassing all others. No other action of the Church can match
its claim to efficacy, nor equal the degree of it.

8. In the earthly liturgy, by way of foretaste, we share in that heavenly liturgy which is celebrated in the holy city of Jerusalem toward   135
which we journey as pilgrims, and in which Christ is sitting at the
right hand of God, a minister of the sanctuary and of the true tabernacle (cf. Apoc. 21: 2; Col. 3:1; Heb. 8:2); we sing a hymn to the
Lord's glory with all the warriors of the heavenly army; venerating the
memory of the saints, we hope for some part and fellowship with   140
them; we eagerly await the Savior, our Lord Jesus Christ, until He,
our life, shall appear and we too will appear with Him in glory (cf.
Phil. 3:20; Col. 3:4).

---

[16] Another important encyclical of Pius XII, *Mystici Corporis* (1943), stressed
the fact of the Church as Christ's Mystical Body. This has been incorporated
(and in some ways greatly surpassed) by the present Constitution and the
Constitution on the Church.

9. The sacred liturgy does not exhaust the entire activity of the Church. Before people can come to the liturgy they must be called to faith and to conversion: "How then are they to call upon him in whom they have not believed? But how are they to believe him whom they have not heard? And how are they to hear, if no one preaches? And how are men to preach unless they be sent?" (Rom. 10: 14–15).

Therefore the Church announces the good tidings of salvation to those who do not believe, so that all human beings may know the true God and Jesus Christ whom He has sent, and may repent and mend their ways (cf. Jn. 17:3; Lk. 24:27; Acts 2:38). To believers also the Church must ever preach faith and repentance. She must prepare them for the sacraments, teach them to observe all that Christ has commanded (cf. Mt. 28:20), and win them to all the works of charity, piety, and the apostolate. For all these activities make it clear that Christ's faithful, though not of this world, are the light of the world and give glory to the Father in the sight of people.

10. Nevertheless the liturgy is the summit toward which the activity of the Church is directed; at the same time it is the fountain from which all her power flows.[17] For the goal of apostolic works is that all who are made sons and daughters of God by faith and baptism should come together to praise God in the midst of His Church, to take part in her sacrifice, and to eat the Lord's supper.

The liturgy in its turn inspires the faithful to become "of one heart in love"[18] when they have tasted to their full of the paschal mysteries; it prays that "they may grasp by deed what they hold by creed."[19] The renewal in the Eucharist of the covenant between the Lord and humanity draws the faithful into the compelling love of Christ and sets them afire. From the liturgy, therefore, and especially from the

---

[17] This solemn paragraph represents the eve of the Church's official teaching on the Liturgy. It is thus something central, by no means secondary or peripheral.

[18] *Postcommunion in the Easter Vigil Mass and the Mass of Easter Sunday.*

[19] *Collect* (prayer) *of the Mass for Tuesday of Easter Week.*

Eucharist, as from a fountain, grace is channeled into us; and the sanctification of people in Christ and the glorification of God, to which all other activities of the Church are directed as toward their goal, are most powerfully achieved.

11. But in order that the sacred liturgy may produce its full effect, it is necessary that the faithful come to it with proper dispositions, that their thoughts match their words, and that they cooperate with divine grace lest they receive it in vain (cf. 2 Cor. 6:1). Pastors of souls must therefore realize that, when the liturgy is celebrated, more is required than the mere observance of the laws governing valid and licit celebration. It is their duty also to ensure that the faithful take part knowingly, actively, and fruitfully.[20]

12. The spiritual life, however, is not confined to participation in the liturgy. The Christian is assuredly called to pray with his brethren, but he must also enter into his chamber to pray to the Father in secret (cf. Mt. 6:6); indeed, according to the teaching of the apostle Paul, he should pray without ceasing (cf. 1 Th. 5:17). We learn from the same apostle that we must always carry about in our body the dying of Jesus, so that the life of Jesus too may be made manifest in our bodily frame (cf. 2 Cor. 4:10–11). This is why we ask the Lord in the sacrifice of the Mass that, "receiving the offering of the spiritual victim," He may fashion us for Himself "as an eternal gift."[21]

13. Popular devotions of the Christian people are warmly commended, provided they accord with the laws and norms of the Church. Such is especially the case with devotions called for by the Apostolic See.

Devotions proper to individual churches also have a special dignity if they are conducted by mandate of the bishops in accord with customs or books lawfully approved.

175

180

185

190

195

---

[20] This theme of awareness and active participation by the faithful is another basic theme of the Constitution. It reinforces recent papal teaching on the meaning of liturgy.

[21] *Secret* (prayer of the Mass) *for Monday of Pentecost Week.*

200 Nevertheless these devotions should be so drawn up that they harmonize with the liturgical seasons, accord with the sacred liturgy, are in some fashion derived from it, and lead the people to it, since the liturgy by its very nature far surpasses any of them.[22]

II. The Promotion of Liturgical Instruction and Active
205 Participation

14. Mother Church earnestly desires that all the faithful be led to that full, conscious, and active participation in liturgical celebrations which is demanded by the very nature of the liturgy. Such participation by the Christian people as "a chosen race, a royal priesthood, a
210 holy nation, a purchased people" (1 Pet. 2:9; cf. 2:4–5), is their right and duty by reason of their baptism.

In the restoration and promotion of the sacred liturgy, this full and active participation by all the people is the aim to be considered before all else; for it is the primary and indispensable source from
215 which the faithful are to derive the true Christian spirit. Therefore, through the needed program of instruction, pastors of souls must zealously strive to achieve it in all their pastoral work.[23]

Yet it would be futile to entertain any hopes of realizing this goal unless the pastors themselves, to begin with, become thoroughly pen-
225 etrated with the spirit and power of the liturgy, and become masters of it. It is vitally necessary, therefore, that attention be directed, above all, to the liturgical instruction of the clergy.[24]

---

[22] While liturgy is not the whole of the Christian life and does not supplant personal prayer, all devotions must harmonize with its spirit.

[23] Again the emphasis on active and conscious participation by the whole Church. Liturgy is thus not a clerical preserve. Rather, the whole people of God has a priestly function which must not be treated as unimportant.

[24] The Council anticipates the danger that some priests, used to different patterns of thought and behavior, may not grasp the central position of worship. Accordingly, priests and future priests are required to become deeply imbued with the liturgical spirit. This section of the Constitution may, in the practical order, prove the most momentous of all.

III
Appendices

A

A Guide for Written Assignments[1]

1. **Typical Types of Theology Writing Assignments:**

   a. *Shorter, Frequent Papers*: Assignments of short summaries of core points in readings, or written answers to analytic-evaluative questions on class material.

   b. *Research Papers*: Assignments of shorter (6–8 paged) term papers for underclassmen, longer (10–15 paged) term papers for upperclassmen.

2. **Qualities Present in Papers Judged as "Outstanding" ("A"):**

   a. Clearly defined and limited topic or question.

   b. Ample bibliography clearly employed and personally understood and synthesized.

   c. Evidence of serious personal reflection and well-reasoned response.

---

[1] Created by the Department of Theology, Marquette Univeristy, for the "Writing in the Arts and Sciences at Marquette" website: http://academic.mu.edu/aswriting/

    d. Clarity of English prose style for formal, academic papers.

    e. Factual accuracy.

    f. Accurate spelling, proper use of vocabulary and grammar, correct term paper form, and overall presentability.

3. Evidences Recognized as Valid Sources of Argumentation:

    a. Official doctrinal teachings of the religion or church in question.

    b. The sacred Scriptures of the religion or church in question.

    c. Worship texts and practices of the religion or church in question.

    d. Faith witness of heroic religious lives—the "saints."

    e. Writings by recognized theological experts, especially in consensus.

    f. Other documents and events interpreted in light of their historical contexts.

    g. Common consensus of humanity across the ages, especially as enshrined in art and literature ("the classics").

    h. The student's personal experience, especially when corroborating any or all of the above.

4. Citation Conventions Required:

Either the MLA style sheet or the Chicago Manual of Style, depending on the preference of individual instructors.

5. Special "Do's" and "Don'ts":

Do's: Re-write! Be clear, reasoned and direct in your writing. Cut out all verbiage. When appropriate, use section headings and give summaries at the end of sections to clarify your argument.

Don'ts: Do not use pompous, jargonese language. Avoid vague generalities. Beware of arguing from purely subjective feelings. No stream-of-consciousness writing.

B
Internet Theology and Religion Sites

1. **Early Church Texts** *Didache,* Justin, etc.:
   http://www.ccel.org/fathers2/

2. **Ancient and Contemporary Christian Creeds:**
   a. Primitive Baptismal and Biblical Creeds:
      http://www.iclnet.org/pub/resources/text/history/creeds.Bible.txt
   b. Later creeds:
      http://www.iclnet.org/pub/resources/text/history/creeds.later.txt
   c. Creeds of every Christian church:
      http://www.Bible.ca/indexchurches.htm

3. **Complete Texts of some works excerpted in INTRODUCTION TO THEOLOGY:**
   a. The Confessions:
      http://www.ccel.org/a/augustine/confessions/confessions.html

    b. Thomas Aquinas, <u>Summa theologiae</u>:
       http://www.ccel.org/a/aquinas/summa/

    c. Julian of Norwich: *http://www.ccel.org/j/julian/revelations/*

    d. <u>Spiritual Exercises</u>:
       http://www.ccel.org/i/ignatius/exercises/exercises.html

4. **Catholic Sites**:

    a. AlaPadre Catholic Corner
       http://alapadre.net/

    b. New Advent: Catholic Website
       http://www.newadvent.org/

    c. Catholic Liturgy
       http://www.catholicliturgy.com/

    d. Vatican City:
       http://www.vatican.va/

    e. Peter's Net
       http://www.petersnet.net/

    f. Catholic Encyclopedia (1917)
       http://www.newadvent.org/cathen/

5. **Orthodox Site**: *http://www.oca.org/Orthodox-Faith/*

6. **Episcopalian Site**:
   http://www.geocities.com/Athens/Acropolis/5766/anglican.html

7. **Lutheran Sites**: *http://www.worship.on.ca/*
   http://www.lutheranworld.org/
   http://www.elca.org/
   http://www.iclnet.org/pub/resources/text/wittenberg/
   wittenberg-luther.html

8. **Muslim Site**: *http://www.unn.ac.uk/societies/islamic/*

C

Traditional Lists and Prayers

A. SOME TRADITIONAL LISTS:

1. Biblical Patriarchs

Antediluvian fathers of the human race, beginning with Adam; plus Abraham, Isaac, Jacob, and Jacob's 12 sons: Reuben, Simeon, Levi, Judah, Issachar, Zubulun, Joseph, Benjamin, Dan, Naphtali, Gad, and Asher. Acts 2:29 names David a "patriarch" as well.

2. Great Women of the Bible

Eve, Sarah, Rebecca, Rachel, Miriam, Rahab, Deborah, Jael, Ruth, Hannah, Bathsheba, Huldah, Judith, Esther, Mother of 7 Sons in *II Maccabees*, Elizabeth, The Blessed Virgin Mary, Mary Magdalen, Mary and Martha.

3. "The Law and the Prophets"

Symbolically represented by the figures of Moses and Elijah.

4. The Four Major Prophets

Isaiah, Jeremiah, Ezekiel, and Daniel.

5. The Twelve Minor Prophets

Hosea, Joel, Amos, Obadiah, Jonah, Micah, Nahum, Habakkuk, Zephaniah, Haggai, Zechariah, and Malachi.

6. The Twelve Apostles

Peter, James, John, Andrew, Thomas, Matthew (Levi), Bartholomew, Philip, James (the Lesser), Simon the Zealot, Judas son of James (Jude/Thaddeus), Matthias.

7. The Ancient Patriarchates

Jerusalem, Antioch, Rome, Alexandria, and Constantinople.

8. Four Great Fathers of the Eastern Church

Sts. Athanasius, Basil the Great, Gregory of Nazianzen, and John Chrysostom.

9. Four Great Fathers of the Western Church

Sts. Ambrose, Jerome, Augustine, and Gregory I ("the Great").

10. Thirty-three "Doctors of the Church"

Sts. Albert the Great, Alphonsus Liguori, Ambrose, Anselm, Anthony of Padua, Athanasius, Augustine, Basil the Great, Bede the Venerable, Bernard of Clairvaux, Bonaventure, Catherine of Siena, Cyril of Alexandria, Cyril of Jerusalem, Ephraem, Francis de Sales, Gregory Nazianzen, Gregory I ("the Great"), Hilary of Poitiers, Isidore of Seville, Jerome, John Chrysostom, John Damascene, John of the

Cross, Lawrence of Brindisi, Leo I ("the Great"), Peter Canisius, Peter Chrysologus, Peter Damian, Robert Bellarmine, Teresa of Jesus (Avila), Thérèse of Lisieux, and Thomas Aquinas.

11. Ecumenical Councils

1.	325	Nicaea I
2.	381	Constantinople I
3.	431	Ephesus
4.	451	Chalcedon
5.	553	Constantinople II
6.	680–81	Constantinople III
7.	787	Nicaea II
8.	869–70	Constantinople IV
9.	1123	Lateran I
10.	1139	Lateran II
11.	1179	Lateran III
12.	1215	Lateran IV
13.	1245	Lyons I
14.	1274	Lyons II
15.	1311–12	Vienne (France)
16.	1414–18	Constance
17.	1438–45	Ferrara-Florence (1431–38 Basel)
18.	1512–17	Lateran V
19.	1545–63	Trent
20.	1869–70	Vatican I
21.	1962–65	Vatican II

(The Orthodox Church recognizes as truly ecumenical, and therefore binding on itself, only the first seven councils listed above. See Timothy Ware [Bishop Kallistos], *The Orthodox Church*[2] [London, 1993] 251–54.)

12. Popes Through the Centuries

1. St. Peter (32–67)
2. St. Linus (67–76)
3. St. Anacletus (Cletus) (76–88)
4. St. Clement I (88–97)
5. St. Evaristus (97–105)
6. St. Alexander I (105–115)
7. St. Sixtus I (115–125)—also called Xystus I
8. St. Telesphorus (125–136)
9. St. Hyginus (136–140)
10. St. Pius I (140–155)
11. St. Anicetus (155–166)
12. St. Soter (166–175)
13. St. Eleutherius (175–189)
14. St. Victor I (189–199)
15. St. Zephyrinus (199–217)
16. St. Callistus I (217–22)
17. St. Urban I (222–30)
18. St. Pontain (230–35)
19. St. Anterus (235–36)
20. St. Fabian (236–50)
21. St. Cornelius (251–53)
22. St. Lucius I (253–54)
23. St. Stephen I (254–257)
24. St. Sixtus II (257–258)
25. St. Dionysius (260–268)
26. St. Felix I (269–274)
27. St. Eutychian (275–283)
28. St. Caius (283–296)—also called Gaius
29. St. Marcellinus (296–304)
30. St. Marcellus I (308–309)
31. St. Eusebius (April–August 309 or 310)
32. St. Miltiades (311–14)
33. St. Sylvester I (314–35)
34. St. Marcus (January–October 336)
35. St. Julius I (337–52)
36. Liberius (352–66)
37. St. Damasus I (366–83)
38. St. Siricius (384–99)
39. St. Anastasius I (399–401)
40. St. Innocent I (401–17)
41. St. Zosimus (417–18)
42. St. Boniface I (418–22)
43. St. Celestine I (422–32)
44. St. Sixtus III (432–40)
45. St. Leo I (the Great) (440–61)
46. St. Hilarius (461–68)
47. St. Simplicius (468–83)
48. St. Felix III (II) (483–92)
49. St. Gelasius I (492–96)
50. Anastasius II (496–98)
51. St. Symmachus (498–514)
52. St. Hormisdas (514–23)
53. St. John I (523–26)
54. St. Felix IV (III) (526–30)
55. Boniface II (530–32)
56. John II (533–35)
57. St. Agapetus I (535–36)—also called Agapitus I
58. St. Silverius (536–37)
59. Vigilius (537–55)
60. Pelagius I (556–61)
61. John III (561–74)
62. Benedict I (575–79)
63. Pelagius II (579–90)

64. St. Gregory I (the Great) (590–604)

65. Sabinian (604–606)

66. Boniface III (February–November 607)

67. St. Boniface IV (608–15)

68. St. Deusdedit (Adeodatus I) (615–18)

69. Boniface V (619–25)

70. Honorius I (625–38)

71. Severinus (May–August 640)

72. John IV (640–42)

73. Theodore I (642–49)

74. St. Martin I (649–55)

75. St. Eugene I (655–57)

76. St. Vitalian (657–72)

77. Adeodatus (II) (672–76)

78. Donus (676–78)

79. St. Agatho (678–81)

80. St. Leo II (682–83)

81. St. Benedict II (684–85)

82. John V (685–86)

83. Conon (686–87)

84. St. Sergius I (687–701)

85. John VI (701–05)

86. John VII (705–07)

87. Sisinnius (January–February 708)

88. Constantine (708–15)

89. St. Gregory II (715–31)

90. St. Gregory III (731–41)

91. St. Zachary (741–52)

92. Stephen II (March 752)

93. Stephen III (752–57)

94. St. Paul I (757–67)

95. Stephen IV (767–72)

96. Adrian I (772–95)

97. St. Leo III (795–816)

98. Stephen V (816–17)

99. St. Paschal I (817–24)

100. Eugene II (824–27)

101. Valentine (August–September 827)

102. Gregory IV (827–44)

103. Sergius II (844–47)

104. St. Leo IV (847–55)

105. Benedict III (855–58)

106. St. Nicholas I (the Great) (858–67)

107. Adrian II (867–72)

108. John VIII (872–82)

109. Marinus I (882–84)

110. St. Adrian III (884–85)

111. Stephen VI (885–91)

112. Formosus (891–96)

113. Boniface VI (April 896)

114. Stephen VII (896–97)

115. Romanus (August–November 897)

116. Theodore II (November–December 897)

117. John IX (898–900)

118. Benedict IV (900–03)

119. Leo V (July–December 903)

120. Sergius III (904–11)

121. Anastasius III (911–13)

122. Lando (913–14)

123. John X (914–28)

124. Leo VI (May–December 928)

125. Stephen VIII (929–31)

126. John XI (931–35)

127. Leo VII (936–39)

128. Stephen IX (939–42)

129. Marinus II (942–46)

130. Agapetus II (946–55)

131. *John XII (955–63)*

132. *Leo VIII (963–64)*

133. *Benedict V (May–June 964)*

134. *John XIII (965–72)*

135. *Benedict VI (973–74)*

136. *Benedict VII (974–83)*

137. *John XIV (983–84)*

138. *John XV (985–96)*

139. *Gregory V (996–99)*

140. *Sylvester II (999–1003)*

141. *John XVII (June–December 1003)*

142. *John XVIII (1003–09)*

143. *Sergius IV (1009–12)*

144. *Benedict VIII (1012–24)*

145. *John XIX (1024–32)*

146. *Benedict IX (1032–45)*

147. *Sylvester III (January–March 1045)*

148. *Benedict IX (April–May 1045)*

149. *Gregory VI (1045–46)*

150. *Clement II (1046–47)*

151. *Benedict IX (1047–48)*

152. *Damasus II (July–August 1048)*

153. *St. Leo IX (1049–54)*

154. *Victor II (1055–57)*

155. *Stephen X (1057–58)*

156. *Nicholas II (1058–61)*

157. *Alexander II (1061–73)*

158. *St. Gregory VII (1073–85)*

159. *Blessed Victor III (1086–87)*

160. *Blessed Urban II (1088–99)*

161. *Paschal II (1099–1118)*

162. *Gelasius II (1118–19)*

163. *Callistus II (1119–24)*

164. *Honorius II (1124–30)*

165. *Innocent II (1130–43)*

166. *Celestine II (1143–44)*

167. *Lucius II (1144–45)*

168. *Blessed Eugene III (1145–53)*

169. *Anastasius IV (1153–54)*

170. *Adrian IV (1154–59)*

171. *Alexander III (1159–81)*

172. *Lucius III (1181–85)*

173. *Urban III (1185–87)*

174. *Gregory VIII (1187)*

175. *Clement III (1187–91)*

176. *Celestine III (1191–98)*

177. *Innocent III (1198–1216)*

178. *Honorius III (1216–27)*

179. *Gregory IX (1227–41)*

180. *Celestine IV (October–November 1241)*

181. *Innocent IV (1243–54)*

182. *Alexander IV (1254–61)*

183. *Urban IV (1261–64)*

184. *Clement IV (1265–68)*

185. *Blessed Gregory X (1271–76)*

186. *Blessed Innocent V (January–June 1276)*

187. *Adrian V (July–August 1276)*

188. *John XXI (1276–77)*

189. *Nicholas III (1277–80)*

190. *Martin IV (1281–85)*

191. *Honorius IV (1285–87)*

192. *Nicholas IV (1288–92)*

193. *St. Celestine V (July–December 1294)*

194. *Boniface VIII (1294–1303)*

195. *Blessed Benedict XI (1303–04)*

196. *Clement V (1305–14)*

197. *John XXII (1316–34)*

198. *Benedict XII (1334–42)*

199. *Clement VI (1342–52)*

200. *Innocent VI (1352–62)*

201. *Blessed Urban V (1362–70)*

202. *Gregory XI (1370–78)*

203. *Urban VI (1378–89)*

204. *Boniface IX (1389–1404)*

205. *Innocent VII (1406–06)*

206. *Gregory XII (1406–15)*

207. *Martin V (1417–31)*

208. *Eugene IV (1431–47)*

209. *Nicholas V (1447–55)*

210. *Callistus III (1445–58)*

211. *Pius II (1458–64)*

212. *Paul II (1464–71)*

213. *Sixtus IV (1471–84)*

214. *Innocent VIII (1484–92)*

215. *Alexander VI (1492–1503)*

216. *Pius III (September–October 1503)*

217. *Julius II (1503–13)*

218. *Leo X (1513–21)*

219. *Adrian VI (1522–23)*

220. *Clement VII (1523–34)*

221. *Paul III (1534–49)*

222. *Julius III (1550–55)*

223. *Marcellus II (April 1555)*

224. *Paul IV (1555–59)*

225. *Pius IV (1559–65)*

226. *St. Pius V (1566–72)*

227. *Gregory XIII (1572–85)*

228. *Sixtus V (1585–90)*

229. *Urban VII (September 1590)*

230. *Gregory XIV (1590–91)*

231. *Innocent IX (October–November 1591)*

232. *Clement VIII (1592–1605)*

233. *Leo XI (April 1605)*

234. *Paul V (1605–21)*

235. *Gregory XV (1621–23)*

236. *Urban VIII (1623–44)*

237. *Innocent X (1644–55)*

238. *Alexander VII (1655–67)*

239. *Clement IX (1667–69)*

240. *Blessed Innocent XI (1676–89)*

241. *Alexander VIII (1689–91)*

242. *Innocent XII (1691–1700)*

243. *Clement XI (1700–21)*

244. *Innocent XIII (1721–24)*

245. *Benedict XIII (1724–30)*

246. *Clement XII (1730–40)*

247. *Benedict XIV (1740–58)*

248. *Clement XIII (1758–69)*

249. *Clement XIV (1769–74)*

250. *Pius VI (1775–99)*

251. *Pius VII (1800–23)*

252. *Leo XII (1823–29)*

253. *Pius VIII (1829–30)*

254. *Gregory XVI (1831–46)*

255. *Ven. Pius IX (1846–78)*

256. *Leo XIII (1878–1903)*

257. *St. Pius X (1903–14)*

258. *Benedict XV (1914–22)*

259. *Pius XI (1922–39)*

260. *Pius XII (1939–58)*

261. *John XXIII (1958–63)*

262. *Paul VI (1963–78)*

263. *John Paul I (August–September 1978)*

264. *John Paul II (1978–)*

13. Seven Gifts of the Holy Spirit

1. Wisdom, 2. Understanding, 3. Counsel, 4. Fortitude, 5. Knowledge, 6. Piety, 7. Fear of the Lord—*Isaiah* 11: 2.

14. Nine Fruits of the Holy Spirit

1. Charity, 2. Joy, 3. Peace, 4. Patience, 5. Kindness, 6. Goodness, 7. Faith, 8. Modesty, 9. Continency—*Galatians* 5:22.

15. Seven Sacraments of the Church

1. Baptism, 2. Confirmation, 3. Eucharist, 4. Holy Orders, 5. Marriage, 6. Reconciliation, 7. Anointing of the Sick.

16. The Roman Calendar
(including saints proper to U.S.A. and S.J.)

Date	Saint or Feast of the Lord (Patron Saint of . . .)	Rank
	First of four Sundays prior to Christmas:	
	FIRST SUNDAY OF ADVENT	Sunday
December 1:	Edmund Campion, S.J., Robert Southwell, S.J., & companions, priests and martyrs	
3:	Francis Xavier, S.J., priest (. . . *all foreign missions, Borneo*)	Memorial
4:	John Damascene, priest and doctor	
6:	Nicholas, bishop (. . . *Russia, merchants, children, sailors, pawnbrokers*)	
7:	Ambrose, bishop and doctor	Memorial
8:	IMMACULATE CONCEPTION (U.S. Holy Day of Obligation) (. . . *the U.S.A.*)	Solemnity
9:	Blessed Juan Diego (U.S.A.)	
11:	Damasus I, pope	
12:	OUR LADY OF GUADALUPE (U.S.A.) (. . . *Mexico, Americas*);	Feast
13:	Lucy, virgin and martyr (. . . *eye diseases*)	Memorial
14:	John of the Cross, O.C., priest and doctor	Memorial
21:	Peter Canisius, S.J., priest and doctor, "The second Apostle of Germany"	
23:	John of Kanty, priest	
25:	CHRISTMAS (U.S. Holy Day of Obligation)	Solemnity
26:	STEPHEN, FIRST MARTYR (. . . *stonemasons*)	Feast

27: JOHN, APOSTLE AND EVANGELIST
(. . . *bookbinders, papermakers*)   Feast

28: HOLY INNOCENTS, MARTYRS (. . . *foundlings*)   Feast

29: Thomas Becket, bishop and martyr

31: Sylvester I, pope

Sunday within octave of Christmas or December 30:
HOLY FAMILY   Feast

January 1: SOLEMNITY OF MARY, MOTHER OF GOD
(U.S. Holy Day of Obligation)   Solemnity

2: Basil the Great and Gregory Nazianzen, bishops and doctors Memorial

4: Elizabeth Ann Seton, religious (U.S.A.)   Memorial

5: John Neumann, C.S.S.R., bishop (U.S.A.)   Memorial

6: EPIPHANY   Solemnity

Sunday after January 6: BAPTISM OF OUR LORD
(End of the Christmas Season)   Feast

7: Raymond of Peñafort, O.P., priest (. . . *canonists*)

13: Hilary of Poitiers, bishop and doctor

17: Anthony, abbot (. . . *skin rashes*)   Memorial

19: Blessed James Sales, S.J., Wm. Saultemouch, S.J.,
Ignatius de Azevedo, S.J., James Bonnarud, S.J.,
Joseph Imbert, S.J., John Cordier, S.J., and S.J.
companions, martyrs

20: Fabian, pope and martyr; Sebastian, martyr
(. . . *lacemakers*)

21: Agnes, virgin and martyr (. . . *chastity*)   Memorial

22: Vincent, deacon and martyr (. . . *vine dressers*)

24: Francis de Sales, bishop and doctor, co-founder of
Order of the Visitation   Memorial

25: CONVERSION OF PAUL, APOSTLE   Feast

26: Timothy and Titus, bishops   Memorial

27: Angela de' Merici, virgin, foundress of the Order
of St. Ursula ("Ursulines")

28: Thomas Aquinas, O.P., "The Angelic Doctor"
(. . . *Catholic schools, theologians*)   Memorial

31: John Bosco, priest, founder of Salesians   Memorial

February 2: PRESENTATION OF OUR LORD   Feast

3: Blase, bishop and martyr; Ansgar, bishop
(. . . *animals, throat diseases*)

5: Agatha, virgin and martyr (. . . *wet nurses, bell founders
and jewelers, fire*)   Memorial

4: John de Brito, S.J., Bl. Rudolph Acquaviva, S.J.,
and companions, priests & martyrs

6: Paul Miki, S.J., and companions, martyrs   Memorial

8: Jerome Emiliani (. . . *orphans and abandoned children*)	
10: Scholastica, virgin	Memorial
11: Our Lady of Lourdes	
14: Cyril, monk; Methodius, bishop; "Apostles of the Slavs" (. . . *Moravia, Europe*)	Memorial
15: Claude de la Columbière, S.J., priest	
17: Seven Founders of the Order of Servites	
21: Peter Damian, O.S.B., bishop and doctor	
22: CHAIR OF PETER, APOSTLE	Feast
23: Polycarp, bishop and martyr	Memorial

Wednesday of the seventh week prior to Easter:

Ash Wednesday, Beginning of THE SEASON OF LENT

March 3: Katharine Drexel, virgin (U.S.A.)	Memorial
4: Casimir (. . . *Poland, Lithuania*)	
7: Perpetua and Felicity, martyrs (. . . *married women*)	Memorial
8: John of God, religious, founder of Brothers Hospitalers (. . . *of the sick and of hospitals*)	
9: Frances of Rome, religious (. . . *motorists*)	
17: Patrick, bishop, "Apostle of Ireland" (. . . *Ireland*)	
18: Cyril of Jerusalem, bishop and doctor	
19: JOSEPH (. . . *the Universal Church, Belgium, a happy death, China*)	Solemnity
23: Turibius de Mongrovejo, bishop	
25: ANNUNCIATION	Solemnity

Sunday after first full moon after vernal equinox:

EASTER SUNDAY	Solemnity with an Octave
April 2: Francis of Paola, hermit, founder of Order of Minim Friars (. . . *seafarers*)	
4: Isidore of Seville, bishop and doctor	
5: Vincent Ferrer, O.P., priest	
7: John Baptist de la Salle, priest, founder of "Christian Brothers"	Memorial
11: Stanislaus, bishop and martyr	
13: Martin I, pope and martyr	
15: Blessed Damien Joseph De Veuster (. . . *people with leprosy*)	
21: Anselm of Canterbury, O.S.B., bishop and doctor	
23: George, martyr, "Protector of England" Adalbert, bishop and martyr (. . . *England, Portugal, soldiers*);	
24: Fidelis of Sigmaringen, O.F.M. Cap., priest and martyr	
25: MARK, EVANGELIST (. . . *notaries*)	Feast
28: Peter Chanel, S.M., priest and martyr; Louis Mary de Montfort, priest	
29: Catherine of Siena, O.P., virgin and doctor (. . . *Italy*)	Memorial

May 1: Joseph the Worker (. . . *laborers, carpenters*)

  2: Athanasius, bishop and doctor, "Father of Orthodoxy"   Memorial

  3: PHILIP AND JAMES, APOSTLES   Feast

  4: Bl. Joseph Rubio, S.J., priest, martyr

 12: Nereus and Achilleus, martyrs (. . . *Roman soldiers*)

    Pancras, martyr

 14: MATTHIAS, APOSTLE   Feast

 15: Isidore the Farmer (married) (U.S.A.) (. . . *Madrid*)

 16: Andrew Bobola, S.J., priest, martyr

 18: John I, pope and martyr

 20: Bernardine of Siena, O.F.M., priest (. . . *advertising*)

 25: Venerable Bede, O.S.B., doctor; Gregory VII, O.S.B.,

    pope; Mary Magdalene de Pazzi, virgin

 26: Philip Neri, priest, founder of Congregation of the Oratory   Memorial

 27: Augustine of Canterbury, O.S.B., bishop,

    "Apostle of the English"

 31: VISITATION   Feast

The fortieth day of Easter: ASCENSION THURSDAY

    (U.S. Holy Day of Obligation)   Solemnity

The fiftieth day of Easter:

    PENTECOST SUNDAY (End of Easter Season)   Solemnity

First Sunday after Pentecost: HOLY TRINITY   Solemnity

Sunday after Holy Trinity: CORPUS CHRISTI   Solemnity

Friday following Second Sunday after Pentecost:

    SACRED HEART (. . . *Ecuador*)   Solemnity

Saturday following Second Sunday after Pentecost:

    Immaculate Heart of Mary   Memorial

June 1: Justin, martyr   Memorial

  2: Marcellinus and Peter, martyrs

  3: Charles Lwanga and companions, martyrs (. . . *Uganda*)   Memorial

  5: Boniface, O.S.B., bishop and martyr, "Apostle of Germany"   Memorial

  6: Norbert, bishop, founder of the Norbertines

    (. . . *Premonstratensians*)

  9: Ephraem the Syrian, deacon and doctor;

    Bl. Joseph de Anchieta, S.J., priest

 11: Barnabas, Apostle   Memorial

 13: Anthony of Padua, O.F.M., priest and doctor

    (. . . *lost objects*)   Memorial

 19: Romuald, abbot, founder of Camaldolese Benedictines

 21: Aloysius Gonzaga, S.J., religious (. . . *youth*)   Memorial

 22: Paulinus of Nola, bishop; John Fisher, bishop

    and martyr; Thomas More, (married) martyr

 24: BIRTH OF JOHN THE BAPTIST (. . . *tailors*)   Solemnity

27: Cyril of Alexandria, bishop and martyr

28: Irenaeus, bishop and martyr — Memorial

29: PETER AND PAUL, APOSTLES (Paul:. . . *ropemakers*) — Solemnity

30: First Martyrs of the Church of Rome

July 1: Blessed Junipero Serra, priest (U.S.A.)

2: Bernadino Realino, S.J., Francis Regis, S.J.,
Francis Jerome, S.J., Bl. Julian Maunoir, S.J.,
Bl. Anthony Baldinucci, S.J., priests

3: THOMAS, APOSTLE (. . . *East Indies, masons*) — Feast

4: Elizabeth of Portugal, religious

5: Anthony Zaccaria, priest

6: Maria Goretti, virgin and martyr

11: Benedict, abbot, founder of O.S.B., "Father of Western
Monasticism" (. . . *Europe*) — Memorial

13: Henry (II, Holy Roman Emperor),
(. . . *Benedictine Oblates*)

14: Bl. Kateri Tekakwitha, virgin (U.S.A.) — Memorial

15: Bonaventure, O.F.M., bishop and doctor,
"The Seraphic Doctor" — Memorial

16: Our Lady of Mount Carmel

18: Camillus de Lellis, priest (. . . *the sick and of their nurses*)

21: Laurence of Brindisi, O.F.M. Cap., priest and doctor

22: Mary Magdalene (. . . *reformed prostitutes*) — Memorial

23: Bridget of Sweden, religious,
foundress of "Bridgettines" (. . . *Sweden*)

25: JAMES (the Greater), APOSTLE (. . . *Spain, Chile*) — Feast

26: Joachim and Ann (Ann:. . . *houseworkers,
cabinet makers, Canada*) — Memorial

29: Martha (. . . *housewives, cooks*) — Memorial

30: Peter Chrysologus, bishop and doctor

31: Ignatius of Loyola, priest, founder of Society of Jesus
("Jesuits") (S.J. SOLEMNITY) — Memorial

August 1: Alphonsus Liguori, bishop and doctor, founder
of C.S.R. ("Redemptorists") — Memorial

2: Eusebius of Vercelli, bishop; Peter Julian Eymard,
priest; Bl. Peter Faber, S.J., priest

4: John Baptist Vianney, priest (. . . *parish priests*) — Memorial

5: Dedication of the Basilica of Saint Mary Major

6: TRANSFIGURATION OF THE LORD — Feast

7: Sixtus II, pope and martyr, and companions, martyrs;
Cajetan, priest, founder of Theatines

8: Dominic, priest, founder of Order of Preachers
("Dominicans") — Memorial

10: LAURENCE, DEACON AND MARTYR (. . . *Sri Lanka*)	Feast
11: Clare, virgin, foundress of Poor Clares (. . . *television*)	Memorial
13: Pontian, pope and martyr, and Hippolytus, priest and martyr	
14: Maximilian Mary Kolbe, O.F.M., priest, martyr	Memorial
15: ASSUMPTION of B.V.M. (. . . *India, airplane pilots*) (U.S. Holy Day of Obligation)	Solemnity
16: Stephen of Hungary (king) (. . . *Hungary*)	
18: Jane Frances de Chantal, religious; Bl. Albert Hurtado Cruchaga, S.J., priest	
19: John Eudes, Orat., priest, founder of Society of Jesus and Mary ("Eudists")	
20: Bernard, O.S.B., Cist., abbot and doctor	Memorial
21: Pius X, pope	Memorial
22: Queenship of the Blessed Virgin Mary	Memorial
23: Rose of Lima, O.P., virgin (. . . *South America; Americas*)	
24: BARTHOLOMEW, APOSTLE	Feast
25: Louis IX (king); Joseph Calasanz, priest	
27: Monica	Memorial
28: Augustine of Hippo, bishop and doctor	Memorial
29: Beheading of John the Baptist, martyr	Memorial
September 3: Gregory (I) the Great, pope and doctor (. . . *singers and scholars*)	Memorial
7: Stephen Pongrácz, S.J., Melchior Grodziecki, S.J., Mark Krizevcanin, S.J., priests, martyrs	
8: BIRTH OF MARY	Feast
9: Peter Claver, S.J., priest (U.S.A.)	Memorial
10: Bl. Francis Gárate, S.J., religious	
13: John Chrysostom, bishop and doctor	Memorial
14: EXALTATION OF THE HOLY CROSS	Feast
15: Our Lady of Sorrows	Memorial
16: Cornelius, pope and martyr, and Cyprian of Carthage, bishop and martyr	Memorial
17: Robert Bellarmine, S.J., bishop and doctor	
19: Januarius, bishop and martyr (. . . *volcanic eruptions*)	
20: Andrew Kim Taegon and Paul Chong Hasang and comp., martyrs	Memorial
21: MATTHEW, APOSTLE AND EVANGELIST	Feast
26: Cosmas and Damian (brothers, physicians), martyrs (. . . *medical doctors*)	
27: Vincent de Paul, founder of the Congregation of the Mission (. . . *all charitable societies*)	Memorial

28:	Wenceslaus (duke of Bohemia), martyr (. . . *Bohemia*); Laurence Ruiz & comp., martyrs	
29:	MICHAEL (. . . *Germany*), GABRIEL, AND RAPHAEL, ARCHANGELS	Feast
30:	Jerome, priest and doctor (. . . *students*)	Memorial
October 1:	Thérèse of the Child Jesus, Carmelite, "Co-Protectress of France" (. . . *foreign missions)*	Memorial
2:	Guardian Angels	Memorial
3.	Francis Borgia, S.J., priest	
4:	Francis of Assisi, deacon, founder of Order of Friars Minor (. . . *Italy*)	Memorial
6:	Bl. Diego de San Vitores, S.J., priest, martyr; St. Bruno, priest, founder of Carthusians; Bl. Marie Rose Durocher, virgin (U.S.A.)	
7:	Our Lady of the Rosary	Memorial
9:	Denis, bishop and martyr, (. . . *France*) and companions, martyrs; John Leonardi, priest	
14:	John Ogilvie, S.J., priest, martyr; Callistus I, pope and martyr	
15:	Teresa of Jesus (Avila), O.C.D., virgin and doctor (. . . *Spain*)	Memorial
16:	Hedwig, religious (. . . *Silesia*); Margaret Mary Alacoque, virgin	
17:	Ignatius of Antioch, bishop and martyr	Memorial
18:	LUKE, EVANGELIST (. . . *painters, artists*)	Feast
19:	Isaac Jogues, S.J., John de Brebeuf, S.J., priests, martrys, & companions S.J., martyrs (U.S.A.);	Memorial
20:	Paul of the Cross, priest	
23:	John of Capistrano, O.F.M., priest	
24:	Anthony of Claret, bishop, founder of the "Claretians"	
28:	SIMON AND JUDE (Jude:. . . *hopeless cases*), APOSTLES	Feast
30:	Bl. Dominic Collins, S.J., religious	
31:	Alphonsus Rodríguez, S.J., religious	
November 1:	ALL SAINTS (U.S. Holy Day of Obligation)	Solemnity
2:	ALL SOULS	
3:	Bl. Rupert Mayer, S.J., priest; St. Martin de Porres, O.P., religious	
4:	Charles Borromeo, bishop	Memorial
5:	All Saints and Blessed of the Society of Jesus	
9:	DEDICATION OF THE BASILICA OF SAINT JOHN LATERAN	Feast
10:	Leo (I) the Great, pope and doctor	Memorial
11:	Martin of Tours, bishop	Memorial
12:	Josaphat, bishop and martyr	

13:	Frances Xavier Cabrini, foundress of Missionary Sisters of the Sacred Heart (U.S.A.)	
	Stanislaus Koska, S.J., religious	Memorial
14:	Joseph Pignatelli, S.J., priest	
15:	Albert the Great, O.P., bishop and doctor, "The Universal Doctor" (. . . *students*)	
16:	Margaret of Scotland (queen); Gertrude the Great, O.S.B., virgin; Roch Gonzalez, S.J., priest & companions, martyrs	
17:	Elizabeth of Hungary (queen), religious	Memorial
18:	Dedication of the Basilicas of Peter and Paul, apostles; Rose Philippine Duchesne, virgin (U.S.A.)	
21:	Presentation of Blessed Virgin Mary	Memorial
22:	Cecilia, virgin and martyr (. . . *musicians*)	Memorial
23:	Clement I, P.M.; Columban, abbot; Bl. Miguel Augustín Pro, S.J., priest and martyr (U.S.A.)	
24:	Andrew Dung-Lac, priest and companions, martyrs	Memorial
26:	John Berchmans, S.J., religious	
30:	ANDREW, APOSTLE (. . . *Scotland, Russia and Greece, fishermen*)	Feast
	Last Sunday in Ordinary Time: CHRIST THE KING	Solemnity

17. Theological Virtues

Faith, Hope, and Charity (Love)

18. Moral or Cardinal Virtues

Prudence, Justice, Temperance, and Fortitude

19. Ten Commandments (Catholic Listing)

I, the Lord, am your God.

1. You shall not have other gods besides me.

2. You shall not dishonor the name of the Lord.

3. Remember to keep holy the Sabbath day.

4. Honor your father and your mother.

5. You shall not kill.

6. You shall not commit adultery.

7. You shall not steal.

8. You shall not bear false witness against your neighbor.

9. You shall not covet your neighbor's spouse.

10. You shall not covet your neighbor's goods.

20. Six Commandments of the Church

1. To assist at Mass on all Sundays and holy days of obligation.

2. To fast and abstain on the days appointed.

3. To confess our sins at least once a year.

4. To receive Holy Communion during the Easter time.

5. To contribute to the support of the Church.

6. To observe the laws of the Church concerning marriage.

(*Taken from: The New Baltimore Catechism, No. 2*)

21. Seven Corporal Works of Mercy

1. To feed the hungry
2. To give drink to the thirsty
3. To clothe the naked
4. To shelter the homeless
5. To visit the imprisoned
6. To visit the sick
7. To bury the dead

22. Seven Spiritual Works of Mercy

1. To convert the sinner
2. To instruct the ignorant
3. To counsel the doubtful
4. To comfort the sorrowful
5. To bear wrongs patiently
6. To forgive injuries
7. To pray for the living and the dead

23. Seven Deadly or "Capital" Sins (Inclinations to Evil)

1. Pride, 2. Covetousness, 3. Lust, 4. Anger, 5. Gluttony, 6. Envy, 7. Sloth.

24. Seven Penitential Psalms

Psalms 6, 32, 38, 51, 102, 130, 143.

25. Four Last Things

Death.   Judgment.   Heaven.   Hell.

B. SOME TRADITIONAL PRAYERS

1. Shema (oldest Jewish prayer)

Hear, O Israel, the Lord is our God, the Lord is One.
Blessed be the name of his glorious majesty forever and ever.

You shall love the Lord your God with all your heart, and with all your soul, and with all your might. And these words which I command you today shall be in your heart. You shall teach them diligently to your children, and you shall speak of them when you are sitting at home and when you go on a journey, when you lie down and when you rise up. You shall bind them for a sign on your hand, and they shall be for frontlets between your eyes. You shall inscribe them on the doorposts of your house and on your gates (*Deuteronomy* 6:4–9).

2. Liturgy of St. John Chrysostom <u>Monogenēs</u> Prayer (Eastern Church)

Only begotten Son and Word of God, Thou who art immortal, and didst deign for our salvation to become incarnate of the holy Theotokos and Ever-virgin Mary, without change becoming man, and Who wast crucified, O Christ God, trampling down death by death: Thou Who art one of the Holy Trinity, glorified together with the Father and the Holy Spirit, save us.

3. A General Confession (Anglican/Episcopalian)

Almighty and most merciful Father; we have erred, and strayed from thy ways like lost sheep. We have followed too much the devices and desires of our own hearts. We have offended against thy holy laws. We have left undone those things which we ought to have done; And we have done those things which we ought not to have done; And there is no health in us. But thou, O Lord, have mercy upon us, miserable offenders. Spare thou those, O God, who confess their faults. Restore thou those who are penitent; According to thy promises declared unto mankind In Christ Jesus our Lord. And grant, O most merciful Father, for his sake; That we may hereafter live a godly, righteous, and sober life. To the glory of thy holy Name. Amen.

4. A General Thanksgiving (Lutheran)

Almighty God, Father of all mercies, we your unworthy servants give you humble thanks for all your goodness and loving-kindness to us and to all whom you have made. We bless you for our creation, preservation, and all the blessings of this life; but above all for your immeasurable love in the redemption of the world by our Lord Jesus Christ, for the means of grace, and for the hope of glory. And, we pray, give us such an awareness of your mercies that with truly thankful hearts we may show forth your praise, not only with our lips, but also in our lives, by giving up ourselves to your service, and by walking before you in holiness and righteousness all our days; through Jesus Christ our Lord, to whom, with you and the Holy Spirit, be honor and glory throughout all ages.

5. A Prayer of Susanna Wesley (Methodist)

You, O Lord, have called us to watch and pray. Therefore, whatever may be the sin against which we pray, make us careful to watch against it, and so have reason to expect that our prayers will be

answered. In order to perform this duty aright, grant us grace to preserve a sober, equal temper, and sincerity to pray for your assistance.
Amen.

6. Prayers of the Rosary:

The Sign of the Cross
†In the Name of the Father, and of the Son, and of the Holy Spirit.
Amen.

The Apostles' Creed
I believe in God the Father Almighty, Creator of Heaven and Earth,
and in Jesus Christ, His only Son, our Lord, Who was conceived by
the Holy Ghost, born of the Virgin Mary, suffered under Pontius
Pilate, was crucified, died, and was buried. He descended into hell,
and on the third day He rose again from the dead. He ascended into
Heaven and sits at the Right Hand of God the Father Almighty; from
thence He shall come to judge the living and the dead. I believe in the
Holy Spirit, the Holy Catholic Church, the Communion of Saints,
the forgiveness of sins, the resurrection of the body, and life everlasting. Amen.

The Glory Be
Glory be to the Father, and to the Son, and to the Holy Spirit, as it
was in the beginning, is now, and ever shall be, world without end.
Amen.

The O My Jesus (The Fatima Prayer)
O, my Jesus, forgive us our sins, save us from the fires of Hell, and
lead all souls to Heaven, especially those in most need of Thy mercy.

The Our Father
Our Father, Who art in Heaven, hallowed be Thy Name, Thy Kingdom come, Thy Will be done on Earth as it is in Heaven. Give us this
day our daily Bread, and forgive us our trespasses, as we forgive those
Who trespass against us. And lead us not into temptation, but deliver
us from evil. Amen.

The Hail Mary

Hail Mary, full of grace, the Lord is with thee. Blessed art thou among women, and blessed is the Fruit of thy womb, Jesus. Holy Mary, Mother of God, pray for us sinners now and at the hour of our death. Amen.

The *Salve Regina*

Hail Holy Queen, Mother of Mercy, our life, our sweetness, and our hope. To thee do we cry, poor, banished children of Eve. To thee do we send up our sighs, mourning, and weeping in this vale of tears. Turn, then, most gracious advocate, thine eyes of mercy upon us, and after this our exile show unto us the blessed Fruit of thy womb, Jesus. O clement, O loving, O sweet Virgin Mary. Pray for us, O holy Mother of God, that we may be made worthy of the Promises of Christ.

Let us pray.

Almighty and ever-living God, Who by the cooperation of the Holy Spirit, didst prepare the body and soul of the glorious Virgin-Mother, Mary, to be a fit dwelling for Thy Son, grant that we who rejoice in her memory may be freed by her kindly prayers both from present ills and from eternal death. Through the same Christ our Lord. Amen.

15 Mysteries of the Rosary:

Joyful:	*Sorrowful:*	*Glorious:*
The Annunciation	Jesus condemned to death	Jesus rises from dead
The Visitation	Jesus scourged at the pillar	Jesus ascends to heaven
The Nativity	Jesus crowned with thorns	Descent of H. S. on Apostles
Presentation in Temple	Jesus nailed to the Cross	Mary assumed into heaven
Finding in the Temple	Jesus dies on the Cross	Mary crowned queen of heaven

7. The Angelus (Outside Eastertime)

(Announced by the church bells at 6:00 or 7:00 A.M., Noon, and 6:00 P.M.)

V- The Angel of the Lord declared unto Mary.

R- And she conceived of the Holy Spirit.

Hail Mary . . .

V- Behold the handmaid of the Lord.

R- Be it done unto me according to thy word.

Hail Mary . . .

V- And the Word was made Flesh.

R- And dwelt among us.

Hail Mary . . .

V- Pray for us, O Holy Mother of God.

R- That we may be made worthy of the promises of Christ.

Let us pray:

Pour forth, we beseech Thee, O Lord, Thy grace into our hearts, that we, to whom the Incarnation of Christ, Thy Son, was made known by the message of an Angel, may by His Passion and Cross be brought to the glory of His Resurrection. Through the same Christ our Lord. Amen.

The *Regina Coeli* (Replaces Angelus during Easter)

Queen of Heaven rejoice, Alleluia,

For he whom thou didst deserve to bear, Alleluia,

Has risen as he said, Alleluia.

Pray for us to God, Alleluia.

V. Rejoice and be glad, O Virgin Mary, Alleluia,

R. Because our Lord is truly risen. Alleluia.

Let us pray:

O God, Who by the resurrection of Thy Son, Our Lord Jesus Christ, hast vouchsafed to make glad the whole world, grant, we beseech Thee, that, through the intercession of the Virgin Mary, His Mother, we may attain the joys of eternal life. Through the same Christ Our Lord. Amen.

8. The <u>Memorare</u> of St Bernard

Remember, O most gracious Virgin Mary, that never was it known that anyone who fled to thy protection, implored thy help, or sought thy intercession was left unaided. Inspired by this confidence, I fly unto thee, O Virgin of virgins, my Mother. To thee I come, before thee I stand, sinful and sorrowful. O Mother of the Word Incarnate, despise not my intentions, but in thy mercy, hear and answer me. Amen.

9. The <u>Come Holy Ghost</u>

V.   Come, Holy Ghost, replenish the hearts of Thy faithful,
R.   And enkindle in them the Fire of Thy Divine Love.
V.   Send forth Thy Spirit, and they shall be re-created;
R.   And Thou shalt renew the face of the earth.

Let us pray:

O God, Who by the light of the Holy Spirit didst instruct the hearts of Thy faithful, grant us by that same Spirit a love and relish of what is right and just, and a constant enjoyment of his divine consolations. Through Christ our Lord. Amen.

10. A Blessing Before Meals

Bless us, O Lord, and these Thy gifts, which we are about to receive from Thy bounty, through Christ our Lord. Amen.

11. A Blessing After Meals

We give thee thanks for all Thy benefits, O Almighty God, who lives and reigns forever;

May the souls of the faithful departed, through the mercy of God, rest in peace. Amen.

12. An Act of Faith

O my God, I firmly believe that Thou art one God in three divine Persons: Father, Son, and Holy Ghost. I believe that Thy divine Son became man, died for our sins, and that He will come to judge the living and the dead. I believe these and all the truths which the Church teaches, because Thou hast revealed them, Who can neither deceive nor be deceived. Amen.

13. An Act of Hope

O my God, relying on Thine almighty power and infinite mercy and promises, I hope to obtain pardon of my sins, the Help of Thy Grace, and Life Everlasting through the merits of Jesus Christ, our Redeemer and Lord. Amen.

14. An Act of Love

O my God, I love Thee above all things, with my whole heart and soul, because Thou art all-good and worthy of all love. I love my neighbor as myself for love of Thee. I forgive all who have injured me and ask pardon of all whom I have injured. Amen.

15. An Act of Contrition

O my God, I am heartily sorry for having offended Thee, because I dread the loss of heaven and the pains of hell, but most of all because they offend Thee, my God, Who art all-good and deserving of all love. I firmly resolve, with the Help of Thy Grace, to confess my sins, do penance and amend my life. Amen.

16. Prayer to One's Guardian Angel

Angel of God, my guardian dear, to whom God's love commits me here, ever this day be at my side, to light and guard, to rule and guide. Amen.

17. Morning Prayer

Live, Jesus, live,
>   so live in me,
That all I do
>   be done by Thee.
And grant that all
>   I think and say,
May be thy thought
>   and word today.
>   Amen.

18. A Prayer of St. Patrick

Christ be with us, Christ before us, Christ behind us,
Christ within us, Christ beneath us, Christ above us,
Christ on our right, Christ on our left,
Christ where we lie, Christ where we sit, Christ where we arise,
Christ in the heart of every one who thinks of us,
Christ in every eye that sees us,
Christ in every ear that hears us.
Salvation is of the Lord,
Salvation is of the Christ,
May your salvation, O Lord, be ever with us. Amen.

19. Prayer of St. Francis of Assisi

Lord, make me an instrument of your peace.
Where there is hatred, let me sow love;
where there is injury, pardon;
where there is doubt, faith;
where there is despair, hope;
where there is darkness, light;
and where there is sadness, joy.

Divine Master, grant that I may not so much seek to be consoled
    as to console;
to be understood as to understand;
to be loved as to love.
For it is in giving that we receive;
it is in pardoning that we are pardoned;
and it is in dying that we are born to eternal life.

20. St. Ignatius' Prayer for Generosity

Dearest Lord, teach me to be generous.
Teach me to serve you as you deserve:
To give and not to count the cost;
To fight and not to heed the wounds;
To toil and not to seek for rest;
To labor and not to ask for reward,
Save knowing that I do your holy will. Amen.

21. The Morning Offering

O JESUS
Through the Immaculate Heart of Mary
I offer you my prayers, works, joys and sufferings of this day
For all the intentions of your Sacred Heart,
In union with the Holy Sacrifice of the Mass throughout the world,
In reparation for my sins,
For the intentions of our associates,
And in particular for . . . (the Pope's monthly intention)

D
Glossary

A. D.–(Latin *Anno Domini* = "in the year of the Lord") Christian designation for human history extending from the birth of Christ up to the present time. See Common Era.

Ambrose (ca. 339–397)–A bishop of Milan, saint and Doctor of the Church, whose preaching contributed to St. Augustine's decision to embrace Christianity. A staunch defender of orthodoxy against paganism and Arianism.

anchoress–a female hermit or recluse.

apostle–(Gr. *apostolos* = "one who is sent out") Someone called and sent by God to preach the gospel. Used most often of "the Twelve" of the gospels who witnessed Jesus' earthly life and preaching and were commissioned by the risen Christ to be founders of his church.

Apostolic Succession–According to Catholic faith, the unbroken continuity through history of the God-given ministry of the college of bishops, in union with the bishop of Rome, to teach, safeguard, and celebrate the basic beliefs and practices of the church received from the Apostles, doing so under the guidance of the Holy Spirit.

asceticism–(Gr. *askesis* = "exercise") The practice of a religious discipline directing one's entire life toward intimacy with God and the doing of God's will. It emphasizes self-control in order to combat vices and develop virtues, as well as a moderation in, or complete renunciation of, various facets of customary social life and personal comfort.

B. C.–= "Before Christ:" The Christian designation for that time in human history before the putative date for the birth of Christ.

B. C. E.–= "Before the Common Era:" An alternative designation for "B.C." See Common Era.

bishop–(Anglo-Saxon corruption of Gr. *episcopos* = "overseer") A member of the highest order of ministers in the church, those established through sacramental ordination as successors of the Apostles and entrusted by God with responsibility both for coordinating the charisms of the members of a local church and, in concert with all other bishops, for guaranteeing the unity of faith and practice of the universal church. Thus, *a personal sacramental symbol* of the church's unity of faith and love: "The bishop is in the church and the church is in the bishop" (St. Cyprian of Carthage [ca 210–258]).

catechesis–(Gr. *katēchein* = "to sound in the ear," "to instruct") Originally used to refer to instruction given to catechumens, those being prepared for baptism. It now refers to any instruction in the faith throughout the life of the Christian.

C. E.–See Common Era

Christology–(Gr. *Christos*, translation of Hebrew "*Mashiakh*," meaning "Anointed One") The study of Jesus Christ, his humanity and divinity, and his saving mission.

Common Era (C. E.)–A contemporary alternative designation for "A.D." (see above). The basis for its calculation is the same as "A.D.," i.e., the putative date of the birth of Christ.

consubstantial–(= *consubstantialis*, the Latin translation of the Council of Nicaea's Gr. *homoousios:* "of the same substance or being")

A technical theological term developed to identify the ontological unity of the three Persons of the Blessed Trinity.

covenant –A voluntary bond uniting two or more parties in mutual love and involving some agreed upon common agenda and purpose.

deacon–(Gr. *diakonos* = "servant," "minister") The sacramentally ordained minister in the church third in order to the bishop and priest (presbyter). As personal aides to the bishop deacons were traditionally entrusted with overseeing the church's care for, and distribution of alms to, the poor. In the liturgy deacons accompanied the presiding bishop or priest, oversaw good order in the church, read the Gospel, announced the prayers of the faithful, and distributed the precious Blood of Christ at Communion. Deacons today in the Catholic Church read the Gospel at the Eucharist and, in the absence of a priest, perform baptisms, witness Christian marriages, and preside at Christian burials.

decalogue–(Gr. "ten words" or "statements") The Ten Commandments delivered by God to Moses on Mt. Sinai revealing to the Israelites the basic demands of their God-given human nature for its proper fulfillment, leading ultimately to full human happiness and union with God.

diaspora–(Gr. "dispersion"—the equivalent of the Hebrew, *galuth* or *golah,* meaning "exile.") The scattering of the Israelite/Jewish people from their homeland. Initially applied to deportees under the Assyrian (722 B.C.) and Babylonian (597 B.C.) conquests, it eventually came to designate all Jewish people living outside of Palestine. In Biblical times Diaspora Jews remained in close touch with their home country, paying the Temple taxes and keeping religious observances.

Doctor of the Church–Title given since the Middle Ages to certain theologian saints whose teachings and lives provide the church with a deeper understanding of her faith. Originally applied to Sts. Ambrose, Augustine, Jerome and Gregory I ("the Great"). A complete current list of those proclaimed "Doctors of the Church" appears in the *Optional Supplementary Material* section above.

doctrine–(Latin *doctrina* = "teaching") Any official teaching of the church interpreting her traditional belief in Jesus Christ in a way designed to speak to the world today. Not necessarily an infallible teaching.

dogma–(Gr. "opinion" or "decree") A religious truth that the church has defined as divinely revealed. Every dogma is a doctrine, but not every doctrine is a dogma.

dualism–Any philosophical or religious system holding that all reality originates from or consists in two irreducible principles or gods. E.g., Manichaeism.

ecclesiastic–Someone who speaks for or represents the church in an official way, usually a person with Holy Orders (bishop, priest, or deacon).

ecclesiology–(Gr. from *ekklesia* = "convocation" or "assembly") That branch of theology which studies the church, her origin, nature, structures and mission.

ecumenism –(derived from Gr. *oikoumene* = "the housed [world]") The modern movement across various Christian denominations to unite divided Christianity into the overall unity intended by Christ for his church.

the elect–Those people effectively "chosen" by God for salvation. In the Catholic R.C.I.A., those who are ritually approved at the beginning of Lent for baptism at the Easter Vigil.

encyclical–(Gr. "circular letter") Formal pastoral letter addressed by the pope to the whole Catholic Church, and often to all people of good will, to convey timely teachings and instructions on matters of Christian faith and morals.

eschatology–(Gr. *eskhatos* = "the last") A study of the "*eschata*," the last things; in theology the study of the ultimate destiny both of the individual soul and of the whole created order.

Eucharist–(Gr. *eukharistia* = "thanksgiving") The sacramental celebration of the Paschal Mystery—Christ's Passion, Death and Resurrection—the central worship of the church. In addition to a blessing prayer over bread and wine and a sharing in them (now become the body and blood of Christ), it is also comprised of Scripture readings and additional prayers, and is presided over by an ordained bishop or priest, who normally delivers a homily as well.

exegesis–(Gr. *exegeisthai* = "to draw out or explain") The act of explaining a sacred text. It attempts, among other tasks, to establish what the authors of the Bible intended to say in their original context and to interpret their message so as to allow God to speak through it today in the fullest possible way to contemporary readers.

faith–According to Scripture, that loving trust in God based upon God's wondrous Self—manifestation in creation and his saving deeds in the past. It includes obedience, the readiness to hear and do God's will (*ob-audire* = "listen to"). This ability to believe in God is only possible as part of God's free Self—gift in Christ dwelling within the believer (grace), communicating the saving faith of Jesus himself (see Hebrews 12:1–3), and thus leading to salvation. "Faith" can also refer to *what* is believed, the doctrinal content of faith. Thus Christ, through the Holy Spirit, is both the sharing *source* and the *content* of the church's faith.

Free Church–A term which originated within the 17th century Church of England designating groups that refused to conform to its discipline and liturgical practice: Society of Friends (Quakers), Puritans, Presbyterians and Methodists. Used today to include as well other denominations that are also without highly formal liturgical traditions. E.g., Baptists.

friar–(ME *frere* from Latin *frater* = brother) A member of a mendicant (begging) religious order in the church, vowed to radical poverty and dedicated to preaching and instructing the faithful. E.g., Dominicans, Franciscans.

grace–(Latin *gratia* = "gift;" Gr. *kharis*) God's gift of Self freely given ("uncreated grace") to human beings in a way that transforms them into daughters and sons of God in Christ, endowed with God's own divine life ("created grace"), bringing with it pardon and healing and participation in Christ's saving work in the world.

Hellenized–(Gr. *Hellas* = "Greece"*)* The state of having become Greek or Greek-like in customs, ideals, form, and/or language.

heresy–(Gr. *hairesis* "choice" or "thing chosen") A baptized person's conscious and deliberate rejection of his or her own church's official dogma.

homoousios–(Gr. = "of the same substance") A non-biblical term used at the Council of Nicaea to describe the equal ontological status of Jesus Christ with God the Father. See consubstantial.

Incarnation–(Latin *caro* = "flesh"; hence, "enfleshing") The assumption of a full human nature by the Second Person of the Blessed Trinity with the result that Jesus Christ is, from the first moment of conception, both truly human and fully divine. The central and defining mystery of the Christian faith.

justification–(Gr. *dikaioo* = "to justify:" i.e., "to make holy," "declare righteous," and/or "acquit") The event or process by which sinful human beings are made acceptable to God. See grace.

liturgy–(Gr. *leitourgia* = "a work for or of the people") The official public worship of the church. "Official" here signifies that the texts and rites have been approved by ecclesial authority. Along with *martyria*, Christian witness, and *diakonia*, Christian service, one of the three primary realizations and manifestations of Christian life in the world.

Logos–(Gr. "word," "message," "discourse," "reason") The Word of God, through whom creation was formed independently of any pre-existing matter or substrate (See *Colossians* 1:15–20). Used with reference to the Second Person of the Trinity.

Magisterium–(Latin *magister* = "master, teacher") Within Catholicism: the pope and bishops in union with him, considered either separately or (especially) in unison, in their function as official, sacramentally ordained teachers of the faith of the Catholic Church. "The Ordinary Magisterium" designates their every-day explication of the Catholic faith; "the Extraordinary Magisterium" refers to the pronouncement by the pope alone or in union with the universal episcopate of any point of faith as demanding unconditional assent by all Catholics, that is, as infallible. E.g., The Immaculate Conception of the Blessed Virgin Mary, 1854, Pope Pius IX.

Manichaeism–The complex dualistic religion developed by Manes (c. 216–276), a Persian, on the basis of various gnostic and Judeo-Christian teachings. Severely ascetic, it envisions life as a constant struggle between two eternal principles: the Spirit of God, the source of all good, and the Spirit of Evil, the cause of all evil in the world, usually identified with matter. The end time will bring the final separation between Light and Darkness and the escape of the soul from the body.

Mass–(ME *missae* = "dismissals") A traditional Catholic name for the Eucharist deriving from solemn dismissal rites during and at the end of the Eucharist in which penitents, catechumens and then the faithful were given special blessings. See Eucharist.

Messiah–(*messias* = Gr. translation of Hebrew *Mashiakh*, "Anointed One") The special person spoken of in Old Testament prophecy as the one whom God would appoint from the lineage of David and invest with special powers for the salvation of the Israelite people. The New Testament presents Jesus Christ in his work of salvation as the fulfillment of this prophetic tradition.

modalism–(Latin *modus* = "aspect, facet") The exaggerated emphasis on the oneness of God which reduces the three "Persons" in God to three ways or "modes" in which a mono-personal God acts in the world.

monasticism–(Gr. *monos* = "one, alone") That living of Christian life defined by vows of poverty, celibate chastity, and obedience in order to pursue both one's own salvation and deeper union with God and the salvation of others through prayer and witness to the faith, most often including some form of loving service. The two basic forms of monasticism are that of the *anchorite,* a hermit, and of the *cenobite*, a member of a stable religious community.

numerology–A study in a supposed deeper significance and power of numbers.

parable–A short fictitious story from ordinary life that illustrates in a parallel way a moral attitude or religious truth.

Passion–(Latin *passio* = "suffering,") The saving transition of Jesus through suffering and death into resurrected life. Understood in the ancient church to include the Last Supper in which Jesus symbolized and explicitated the inner freedom and love that animated those saving events.

Neo-Platonism–A revival and religious interpretation of the philosophy of Plato (427?–347 B.C.), developed by Plotinus (A.D. 205–270), which flourished from the third to the sixth century A.D. It teaches that all reality has emanated from "The One," the supreme reality to which human beings must return through purification, knowledge, and love in order to be saved.

patristics–(Latin *pater* = "father") Study of the history and the theology of "the Fathers," those ancient Christian writers, mostly bishops, whom mainstream Christian tradition has always regarded as highly authoritative witnesses to the authentic faith and practice of the church. Historians give various dates for the "Patristic Age," typically beginning with St. Irenaeus (fl. ca. 185) and extending as late as to St. John Damascene (ca. 675–ca. 749).

Pelagianism–A Christian heresy identified with a wandering British monk, Pelagius (ca. 350–425), teaching that human beings can achieve salvation through their own sustained efforts, independently of divine grace. Opposed by St. Augustine and condemned by the Council of Ephesus in A.D. 431.

Platonism–The philosophy of Plato (427?–347 B.C.). It asserts the existence of a higher intelligible world of eternal, changeless, and universal ideas or forms. Physical objects of the sensible world are "real" only to the degree that they image, and thereby participate in, the forms.

pneumatology–(Gr. *pneuma* = "spirit") The branch of theology, developed in the fourth century, which studies the Person and work of the Holy Spirit, the Third Person of the Blessed Trinity.

predestination–(Latin *praedestinare* = "to foreordain") That theological understanding according to which God knows and even foreordains from all eternity which human persons are to be saved.

priest–(Gk. *presbyter* = "elder" → Ger. *priester*) A sacramentally ordained member of a bishop's advisory body, co-responsible with and under him for the guidance and leadership of the church by personal example and teaching of the faith, and by presiding at liturgy. A term which through history came also to translate the Greek *hiereus* = "one who deals with the sacred," i.e., one who offers sacrifice— leading to the mistaken notion that only priests and bishops, and not the assembly as a whole under the leadership of bishop or priest, truly offer the Eucharist.

Providence–(Latin *providere* = "to have foresight," "to provide for") The divine plan by which God lovingly works for the ultimate good of all of creation, including his guiding the course of individual lives.

redaction –The work done by those biblical authors who, in editing earlier textual material, introduced changes according to the messages they wished to communicate to their particular audiences.

redemption–(Latin *redemptio* = "buying back") God's saving activity which delivers humankind from sin and evil into communion with God.

The Reformation–(Latin *reformare* = "to renew, give new form") The religiously motivated movement of the sixteenth century responding to abuses in the Catholic Church by reliance solely on the scriptural word of God. Although not its original intention, it separated large sections of Western Christendom from the institutional Catholic Church and resulted in the establishment of various Protestant ecclesial communions.

retreat–A period of withdrawal—either in a group or individually— for prayer and meditation, often under the guidance of a director.

revelation–(Latin *revelare* = "to take away the veil") God's self-disclosure both through the created world and human events (see Wisdom 13:1–9, Romans 1:20), and in a special, full, and definitive way in the person, words, and actions of Jesus Christ.

righteousness–The state of union with God through grace in which we are acceptable to God.

sacramentals–Sacred symbols of the church's faith through which God manifests and realizes his saving presence but which individually are not, like the seven Sacraments, essential to the church's continuing existence and mission in the world. Examples include: blessings of persons (including the sign of the cross), of meals, and of objects which are thereby set aside for holy activities—such as holy water, metals, palms, rosaries, crucifixes, Ash Wednesday ashes, candles, etc., and officially sanctioned holy activities such as Benediction with the Blessed Sacrament, Stations of the Cross, pilgrimages, etc.

Sacraments–(Latin *sacramentum* = "sacred reality," "oath," "pledge"— The Latin equivalent of Gr. *mysterion* = "mystery," "sacred rite") The essential liturgical rites of the church in which God acts through the church's faith to communicate his divine life to people and through which participants experience the love and power of God (grace) that flows from Christ's passion, death, and resurrection. The Catholic Church officially recognizes and celebrates seven Sacraments: Baptism, Confirmation, Eucharist, Holy Orders, Marriage, Penance/Reconciliation, and Anointing of the Sick.

salvation–(Latin "making safe," "rescuing") Complete and eternal union with God, delivering humanity and all creation from the destructive power of sin and death.

sanctification–(Latin "being made holy," "making holy") The holiness of union with God realized in and through God's self-gift in Jesus Christ ("uncreated grace") to human beings, bringing about interior personal transformation ("created grace"), that which the Eastern church calls "illumination" and "divinization."

schism–A formal institutional division in or separation from a church or religious body.

scholasticism–(Gr. *skholē* "leisure" → Latin *schola* "school") A medieval method of theological inquiry using Aristotelian approaches to ordering and analyzing reality and applying them to the truths of the church's faith. So named because it was developed in the various *schools* maintained in European universities by religious orders (e.g., Dominicans, Franciscans).

Scripture–Sacred writings so inspired by God as to be normative, when taken as a whole, of the faith of the church.

Semi-Pelagianism–A teaching, eventually condemned by the church, first articulated by certain fifth-century monastic theologians who opposed the extreme predestination theology of St. Augustine. Although these theologians did not deny that God's grace is necessary for salvation, they insisted that human beings must make the first step without the help of grace, in order to make themselves open to receive the necessary grace.

Septuagint–(Gr. *septuaginta* "seventy"). A third-century B.C. Greek translation of the Old Testament which, according to legend, was completed in seventy days by seventy translators, each of the entire text, working independently of one another and yet arriving at completely identical results, thereby confirming that their mutually agreeing Greek translations themselves were divinely inspired. Often designated, when cited, by the Roman numerals for seventy: LXX.

soteriology–(Gr. *sōtēr* = "savior") The branch of theology which investigates the church's faith in Christ as Savior of the world.

subordinationism–An understanding of God in which the Son is seen as inferior in divinity to the Father, and the Holy Spirit inferior to both the Son and the Father.

tabernacle–(Latin *tabernaculum* = "tent") The sacred container, normally found in the sanctuaries of church buildings, which holds the consecrated hosts for Holy Communion. It has its origin in the tent in which the Israelites housed the Ark of the Covenant which itself was a sacred receptacle and a kind of throne of the invisible God.

theology–(Gr. *theos* = "God") Literally, the "study of God." It is "faith seeking understanding" (St. Anselm of Canterbury [1033–1109]). It begins with the church's faith and proceeds in methodical ways, developing an organized body of knowledge, to understand and interpret that faith in relationship to contemporary understandings of the world and human life.

tradition–(Gr. *paradosis* → Latin *traditio* = "transmission") Seen from various perspectives as (1) the church's inner *life* in Christ, (2) the *truth content* of that life as manifested in the church's (a) dogmas, (b) ritual worship and (c) customs, and (3) the *process* by which that true life is handed on in the church to each successive generation.

Trinity–The fundamental article of the church's faith in one God in three Persons.

virtue–(Latin *virtus* = "force") A habit of good behavior which enables one to do what is right with increasing ease, joy, and consistency. The opposite of a virtue is a vice, the humanly destructive habit that facilitates our continuing to do evil.

Zion–Originally the fortified hill of pre-Israelite Jerusalem, i.e., the crest of the hill between the Tyropoeon and the Kidron valleys, south of the Temple area. Later (in the Psalms) used to refer to the Temple area. Later still, a name for Jerusalem itself and even the whole ancient Israelite community. In early Christian usage "Zion" named the SW hill of Jerusalem because of the belief that the Apostles gathered there on Pentecost. In Christian allegory, the heavenly city of the just.

E
Theological Index

F

Maps

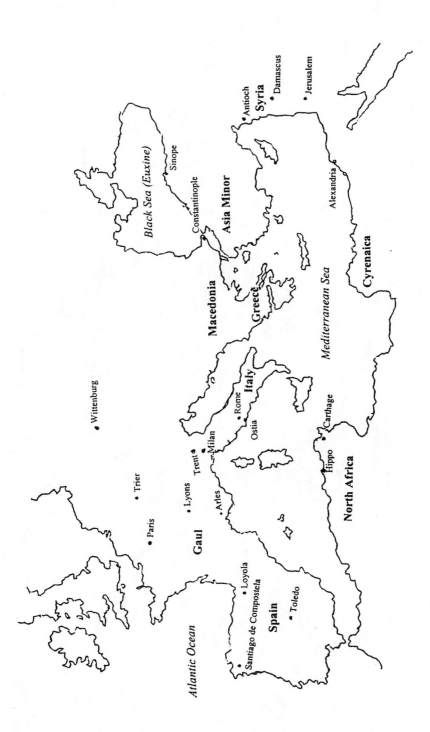

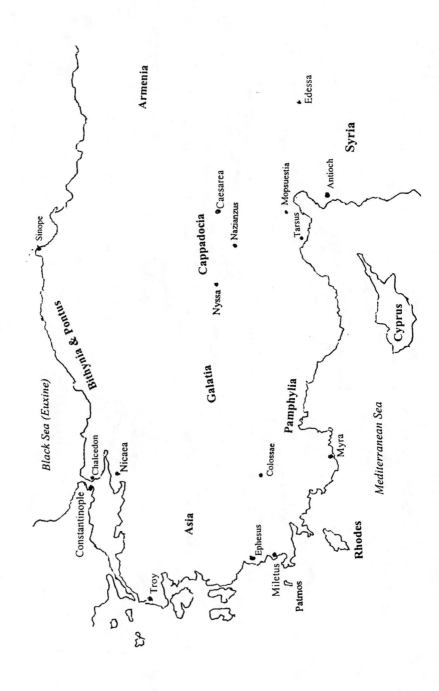

Tyre

Capernaum

Magdala • *Sea of Galilee*

Caesarea •

Nazareth

Galilee

Mediterranean Sea

• Sichar

Samari

Perea

Judea

Jericho •

Emmaus •

Jerusalem

• Bethlehem

Dead Sea

Masada •